Private Landscapes

Modernist Gardens in Southern California

PRINCETON ARCHITECTURAL PRESS

Private Landscapes

Modernist Gardens in Southern California

Pamela Burton
Marie Botnick

Introduction by Kathryn Smith

PRINCETON ARCHITECTURAL PRESS

Published by
Princeton Architectural Press
37 East Seventh Street
New York, New York 10003
www.papress.com
For a free catalog of books, call 1.800.722.6657.

ISBN 1-56898-402-2

Packaged by
Grayson Publishing
James G. Trulove
Washington, DC
jtrulove@aol.com

Art Direction
James Pittman, James Trulove

Printed in Hong Kong

05 04 03 02   5 4 3 2 1 First edition

Library of Congress Cataloging-in-Publication Data

Burton, Pamela.
Private Landscapes: Modernist Gardens in Southern
California/Pamela Burton, Marie Botnick; introduction by
Kathryn Smith.
        p. cm.
        Includes bibliographical references (p. 190).
        ISBN 1-56898-402-2
1. Gardens--California, Southern.
2. Gardens--California, Southern--Design.
3. Landscape Architecture--California, Southern. I.
Botnick, Marie. II. Title.
SB466.U65 C373 2003
712'.6'097949--dc21
                                        2002010638

Contents

The Pavilion in the Garden
Kathryn Smith

Although numerous books have been written about modern architecture in southern California, there is no book devoted solely to the subject of modern landscape design or modernist gardens in the Southland. In fact, the question could be posed, "Did modern houses have gardens?" This confusion exists because of the traditional perception of gardens that extends back through history to the great styles of Italy, France, and Great Britain. One is reminded immediately of the illustrious Renaissance gardens around Florence and Rome such as the Villa Lante; the great Baroque gardens of France, Versailles and Vaux-le-Vicomte; or incomparable Sissinghurst in England. All of these celebrated landscape masterworks have been imitated in southern California for the grand estates of Hollywood and Montecito; but amid these lavish horticultural displays are the more modest examples of an original style of landscape, one that arose from the conditions of the twentieth century: modernism.

Although modernism is generally regarded as a European movement, there is a strong and independent tradition in southern California that can be traced back to as early as 1911 in the work of Irving Gill, a startlingly original innovator. And from Gill, there is a direct connection to seminal buildings of the 1920s and 1930s by the Austrian emigrés, Rudolph M. Schindler and Richard J. Neutra. By the time the post World War II building boom was over, southern California could boast the largest concentration of modern houses in the world. In addition to Schindler and Neutra, other modernists included J.R. Davidson, Gregory Ain, Harwell Hamilton Harris, Raphael Soriano, Rodney Walker, Thornton Abell, Joseph van der Kar, Lloyd Wright, John Lautner, Craig Ellwood, Pierre Koenig, Frederick E. Emmons and A. Quincy Jones. These architects all shared a common approach that combined modern forms with a distinct understanding and sympathy for the natural site and its particular characteristics of terrain and vistas. It was this approach more than anything else that distinguished these architects from their European contemporaries—Walter Gropius, Mies van der Rohe, Le Corbusier, and Hannes Meyer. By addressing the site, they located their buildings within nature, as opposed to separate from it. As a result of this singular viewpoint, it was in southern California that modern residential architecture realized its ideal: the house as the pavilion in the garden replacing the traditional Western view of a house as shelter—a massive and solid dwelling—isolated and protected from a harsh and threatening environment.

From the beginning, modern architects in southern California designed their own landscaping and created gardens for their clients' houses. This changed at the end of World War II when the landscape architect Garrett Eckbo moved to Los Angeles and was quickly accepted as an equal collaborator by Ain, van de Kar, and Jones as well as by numerous other architects. Between 1945 and 1965, Eckbo established the tenets of modern landscape architecture in southern California. With his mature style, he extended architectural means into the garden through the use of devices such as pergolas, trellises, and angled or curving walls, often employing industrial materials such as metal and plastics. If there is any single practitioner who can be identified with modern landscape architecture as a professional discipline in southern California, it certainly is Eckbo, who left a legacy of hundreds of gardens throughout the region. It is clear by examining Eckbo's work that landscape concepts in southern California often differed in attitude and vocabulary from elsewhere in the United States and, certainly, from Europe. As a result, it is impossible, even with Eckbo, to isolate the most distinctive gardens of modern houses from a regional lifestyle and the native landscape.

Modern Architecture: Inside-Outside

In the period before World War I, southern California gardens usually made references to the past: either the local Spanish tradition of walled courtyards or the imported style of Victorian gardens emulating the English ideals of the picturesque. For large and expensive homes in the historic styles of Italy and France, elaborate formal gardens flourished in the mild climate conducive both to evergreen foliage and year-round floral abundance. The exclusive communities of Pasadena, San Marino, and Montecito were the locations for enormous estates—with names like Val Verde or La Toscana—landscaped by designers such as Florence Yoch, A.E. Hanson, Edward Huntsman-Trout, and Lockwood de Forest.

Modernism was not imported to the region; it emerged with the buildings of Irving Gill, who arrived in San Diego in 1893 after working for two years in the Chicago office of Louis Sullivan and Dankmar Adler. Coincidentally Frank Lloyd Wright, who built several important houses in Los Angeles in the 1920s, was an employee in the same office during those years. It was Sullivan who ultimately would have the most decisive influence over the direction of the modernist garden in southern California. Echoing Transcendentalist writers such as Ralph Waldo Emerson and Henry David Thoreau, Sullivan held that nature provided a moral benefit in an increasingly industrialized world. To maintain mental and physical health, it was imperative to have a personal relationship to the natural world. Sullivan's conviction—that architects should serve as the mediating force between people and nature—was passed on to both Gill and Wright. This philosophical attitude distinguishes Sullivan, Wright, and Gill from their European counterparts—Peter Behrens, Le Corbusier, and Gropius—whose Cartesian distance from nature created a negative response to landscape as expressed in Le Corbusier's famous slogan, "a house is a machine for living." While the Europeans were focused on designing houses that both looked like and could be built like machines for mass production (buildings conceived as objects that were alien to their context), L.A. modernists created houses that grew up from and embraced their sites.

The physical beauty of California was the perfect foil for Gill's pure cubic abstraction. "The intense blue of sky and sea that continues for such long, unbroken periods, the amethyst distant mountains, the golden brown of summer fields, the varied green of pepper, eucalyptus, and poplar trees," Gill claimed, was the ideal setting for his houses.[1] Courtyards, terraces and pergolas served as connections between the house and garden and achieved the interpenetration of indoor and outdoor space that Gill admired in the historic mission architecture of early California. In plan, Gill preferred a house that was a "walled garden"—U-shaped around a court—providing year-round outdoor living for the family, especially the children.

"We should build our house simple, plain and substantial as a boulder," Gill declared in 1916, "then leave the ornamentation of it to Nature, who will tone it with lichens, chisel it with vines and flower shadows as she does the stone in the meadow."[2] To realize this goal, Gill worked, on occasion, with the well-known San Diego horticulturist, Kate O. Sessions, who was sympathetic to his interest in developing a style suited to the genius loci—the genius of the place. Responding to Gill's desire to create "a simple cube house with creamy walls, sheer and plain, rising boldly into the sky—unornamented save for the vines that soften a line or creepers that wreathe a pillar," Sessions drew from a palette of plant materials suited to the climate of southern California. She preferred vines such as the rosy-crimson passion flower (Passiflora racemosa), mandevillas, and several of the bougainvilleas.

Just as Gill's career was coming to a close, Frank Lloyd Wright received a large commission that brought him to Hollywood. It was Wright even more than Gill who served as the link between Sullivan and the nascent group of modern architects who would settle in Los Angeles in the 1920s. The Prairie Houses of the Midwest (1900–10) had brilliantly demonstrated Wright's power to translate landscape into architectural metaphor. Between 1919 and 1923, he would be occupied in renewing his vocabulary in response to southern California. If Wright was profoundly repelled by the proliferation of historic styles of building he saw all around him in Los Angeles, he was deeply inspired by the poetic qualities of the natural terrain. "Curious tan-gold foothills rise from tattooed sand-stretches," he observed, "to join slopes spotted as the leopard-skin with grease-bush. This foreground spreads to distances so vast—human scale is utterly lost as all features recede, turn blue, recede and become bluer still to merge their blue mountain shapes, snow-capped, with the azure of the skies."[3]

Wright's work in Los Angeles was divided into two periods: the first was devoted to Aline Barnsdall, who had purchased Olive Hill, a 36 acre site in Hollywood, planted

Irving Gill, Miltmore House, 1911. Front entry pergola covered with wisteria vine.

with an orchard of olive trees, commanding panoramic views of mountains, ocean and the city. In a second period, from 1923–24, he designed and built a series of houses on the hillsides and in the canyons in concrete construction, which he called "textile block." Olive Hill was one of his first major landscape commissions which went far beyond the Prairie House in its ambitions. With the Prairie House, Wright had created a tight integration of landscape features with built forms by extending the geometry of the house into the garden, resulting in a formal plan. Typical of these houses, the building reaches out into sheltered courts, broad terraces, formal pools and geometric planting beds. The building and its gardens form an integrated unity.

Wright began abandoning this pattern after his move to California as he sought to place his buildings in an ideal setting. The character-defining elements of Olive Hill fit precisely Wright's view of the archetype, with its elevation raised above the floor of Hollywood; its vistas of sea, mountains, and sky; and its orthogonal grid of olive groves representing a pastoral connection to nature.

Olive Hill was one of the largest landscape designs Wright had executed up to that date; and in this project he collaborated with his son, Lloyd Wright, who had experience as a landscape designer. After only a year of college, Lloyd Wright obtained a job as a draftsman with the well-respected office of Olmsted and Olmsted in Boston (successor firm to the famous Frederick Law Olmsted, founding father of American landscape architecture). It was in this position that he traveled to San Diego in 1911 to work in the nursery created to grow plant material for the Panama California International Exhibition. From 1912–15, he was employed by Irving Gill. While in this office, he worked on the landscaping for the new industrial city of Torrance, a joint project of Gill and Olmsted and Olmsted. By 1915, he had formed a partnership with Paul Thiene as landscape architects with a practice devoted primarily to large estates. During these years, Lloyd Wright became familiar with non-native species that originated in areas such as the Mediterranean, Australia, or South Africa. His choice was for specimens such as eucalyptus, acacias, cedars, and cypress that would do well in the semi-arid climate of southern California. In this sense, Lloyd Wright could be compared to his contemporaries: Yoch, Huntsman-Trout, and Lockwood de Forest.

The most influential garden design on Olive Hill was the elder Wright's concept for the main residence, Hollyhock House, named after Barnsdall's favorite flower, which grew wild on the hills of her site. The house, with a U-shaped plan, was integrated with a series of pools, terraces, and an interior patio that began to blur the distinction between inside and outside. At the boundary between the living room loggia and the interior patio, Wright introduced an unusual feature: two accordion-folding glazed doors. When these were pushed to each side, the garden entered into the house through the loggia, a transitional zone between the patio and the main public rooms. The idea was further reinforced by planters built into the corners of the doorway leading to the living room. Despite these innovations, the Hollyhock House was governed by traditional elements such as a strong central axis so that symmetry became the overriding principle in the garden.

Frank Lloyd Wright, Hollyhock House, 1919–21. View of interior courtyard with lily pond.

With the Hollyhock House and textile block houses such as the Millard House in Pasadena, Wright gave architectural expression to Sullivan's philosophy of integrating man and nature. Yet Wright's influence on modernist gardens in southern California was two-fold. It was because of him that Schindler and Neutra, two important modern architects, came to Los Angeles. Schindler entered Wright's studio in 1918 and came to Hollywood in December 1920 to supervise construction of the Hollyhock House. Neutra followed in 1925, after spending several months as an apprentice with Wright at his Wisconsin studio-residence, Taliesin. If Los Angeles was still dominated by historical styles when they arrived, by the end of the 1930s, Schindler and Neutra had completed a number of commissions that would firmly establish modernism in Los Angeles.

Architecture and Space—Gardens and Space

For Schindler and Neutra, there were two major sources for new design ideas: their European background and their American experience. As early as 1912 while still in Vienna, Schindler had written, "The architect has finally discovered the medium of his art: S P A C E." His European preference for intersecting volumes of space and a commitment to geometric abstraction were reinforced by exposure to Wright.

By 1926, Schindler's radical ideas about modern living and design were circulated to the general public when he authored a series of articles in the *Los Angeles Times*. In "Shelter or Playground," the last of six essays, Schindler declared that landscape would take on greater importance in the future: "Our rooms will descend close to the ground and the garden will become an integral part of the house. The distinction between the indoors and the out-of-doors will disappear." Schindler had demonstrated this idea directly in 1921 in his first independent design, a double residence for himself, his wife, and another couple, Clyde and Marian Chace. In this building, its architect created a composition in which walls, floor and roof defined, but did not contain, space. The idea was continued in the garden where Schindler created a series of discrete rooms by using bamboo hedges and ornamental grasses for overlapping horizontal planes. A subtle manipulation of ground planes

(sunken gardens placed strategically) indicates that Schindler conceived of the garden in terms of spatial volumes rather than as pattern. The building and the garden were continuations of each other; modern architecture had moved into the landscape.

These developments were well known to Neutra, who lived at the Schindler House with his family for five years between 1925 and 1930. Neutra, who worked in Switzerland and Germany after the First Word War, was an important connection between modernism in Europe and the ideas of Sullivan and Wright in America. In addition to his training as an architect, in 1919 Neutra apprenticed to the landscape architect, Gustav Ammann, in Otto Froebel's nursery in Zurich. This was a formative experience for Neutra and would distinguish him from other members of his generation such as Gropius or Mies. Even though the two years (1921–23) he spent in the office of Erich Mendelsohn immersed him in the tenets of European modernism, while there he continued his work in landscaping by assisting on the Einstein Tower in Potsdam.

Neutra arrived in Chicago in 1924 and met Louis Sullivan shortly before he died. Neutra's first meeting with Wright occurred at Sullivan's funeral, though Schindler had been trying for years to get him a job in Wright's studio. Neutra traveled to Wisconsin in late 1924 to spend several months as an apprentice; but Wright had little work. In February 1925, Neutra left for Los Angeles. One of his first jobs after being invited to move into Schindler's studio-residence was executing the landscape plans for several of Schindler's commissions, including the Lovell House in Newport Beach (1922–26).

While Neutra clearly designed in the International Style as European modernism was dubbed (he was one of the few Americans exhibited by the Museum of Modern Art in their 1932 landmark exhibit of the same name), his apprenticeship with Ammann and his exposure to Sullivan and Wright obviously shaped his own unique perspective. In a 1951 book, *Mystery and Realities of the Site*, he expressed his commitment to a site-specific approach rather than a standardized solution often identified with Gropius and the philosophy of his famous design school, the Bauhaus. In an astonishing departure from his European contemporaries, Neutra stated, "My experience, everything within me, is against an abstract approach to land and nature, and for the *profound assets rooted in each site* and buried in it like a treasurable wonder. The ancients thought those vital assets spirits. By listening intently, you can hear them miraculously breathe in their slumber. You may subtly awaken them to startling values of design truly assured of duration, growth, and never-ending life." (Neutra's italics)

By the end of the 1930s, it was clear that modern houses in southern California were different from their counterparts in Europe in one important respect: their sensitive relationship to their site, and, as a consequence, their landscaping. There were two major factors that influenced this direction in a pragmatic way. First, the Mediterranean climate of warm winters and dry summers, and secondly, the desire to live outdoors as much as possible whenever the weather permitted. In addition, changing social and economic conditions meant that architects were designing for smaller lots, families without servants, and a more informal lifestyle with an emphasis on recreation and exercise. By the time Davidson, Ain, Harris, and Soriano started out with their own clients, there was already a set of unwritten principles for modernist gardens established through the work of Schindler and Neutra:

1. The rejection of historical models in favor of the treatment of plants as abstract sculptural forms.
2. Treatment of the garden as a spatial composition rather than as a composition of decorative surface patterns.
3. The use of multiple viewpoints and diagonal paths as ordering devices rather than the use of a central axis which produced symmetry.
4. Low-maintenance gardens that emphasized texture and drought-tolerant plants over floral display.
5. The use of an architectural framing device to introduce "borrowed scenery."
6. The increased intimacy of house and garden through walls of plate glass, sliding doors, and the use of the same surface material for the floor of house and patio.

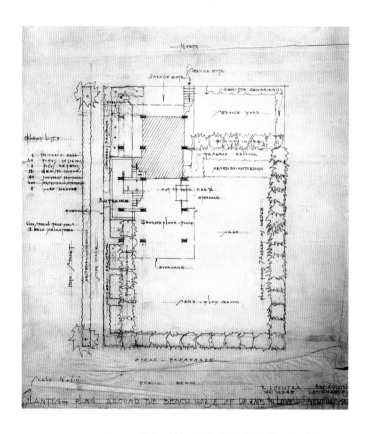

Richard Neutra for R.M. Schindler, Lovell House, landscape plan, c. 1925–26.

Richard Neutra, Singleton House, 1959. The garden and house are a spatial continuum through walls of glass.

7. The garden conceived as an "outdoor room" for recreation and sports (with, by 1950, the swimming pool as a major focal point) rather than as decoration to be viewed passively.

The Second Generation

With the exception of Neutra, whose experience in Mendelsohn's office in Germany was unique, the majority of early modern architects in Los Angeles were not directly shaped by events in Europe. Their knowledge and experience of modernism was gained as a result of their exposure to the architecture and theories of Wright, Schindler and Neutra. For Gregory Ain and Harwell Hamilton Harris, the Schindler House was central to their development for two reasons. The innovations in the house and garden had a profound influence on the ideas of both young architects and it was at the Schindler House that they discovered Neutra. Ain's first visit was in 1924 when he met only Schindler. Harris came by in 1928 and found both architects together (by then they had formed a loose architectural partnership). Schindler's influence was through the example of his house, Neutra's was direct and personal.

Between 1928 and 1930, Neutra forcefully promoted the practice of modern architecture in Los Angeles via an unprecedented campaign of self-propelled activity. He taught a class on modern building at the Academy of Modern Art in Hollywood and from this course gathered together a small group of apprentices—Ain and Harris among them—to execute theoretical designs for a utopian city. Among his proposals were plans for garden apartments for families that united housing and landscaping in new and experimental ways. The noted architectural historian Esther McCoy pointed out in her book, *The Second Generation*, "Thus began one of the most vital and concentrated student projects ever attempted in the United States. It was the more remarkable because it came from a nonaccredited school—a nonschool, in fact—directed by a 33-year old architect with no previous teaching experience, newly licensed, with one completed building and a second almost finished."[4] Both Ain and Raphael Soriano worked briefly for Schindler; more importantly, they were employed by Neutra after he left the Schindler House and moved to a studio-residence of his

13

own design in Silverlake. Ain lived and worked there for two years between 1933–35.

By the middle of the 1930s, there was already a significant concentration of modern houses in Los Angeles. In the decade of 1945–55, which witnessed the most significant explosion in residential building in southern California, it was clearly unnecessary to import the style from Europe.

Mid-century Modernist Gardens

The most significant single event in the history of the modernist garden in southern California was the arrival of Garrett Eckbo in 1946. Part of the trio of great American landscape architects of the twentieth century along with Dan Kiley and James Rose, Eckbo brought a radical new sensibility to garden design. He began his education at Harvard at a crucial moment when the impact of modern art and design from Europe was challenging the status quo of the Beaux-Arts traditionalists. Eckbo realized that the profession of landscape architecture required both formal and social reform. Taking inspiration from abstract painting—especially from the work of Wassily Kandinsky and Joan Miró—Eckbo drew on new visual experiments to revitalize landscape plans with dynamic spatial compositions; geometric shapes such as circles, triangles, and irregular polygons; and a novel color palette of saturated primary colors. Utilizing these novel design ideas, he began to address a wide variety of subjects from small plots for migrant workers to large planning projects.

When he opened a Los Angeles office of Eckbo, Royston, and Williams in 1946, the timing was perfect. The post-war building boom was on. The principles of modern architecture that had been worked out in Los Angeles in the 1920s and 1930s provided a style that was seized upon for post-war housing, whether in the form of large-scale progressive housing tracts or more expensive custom-designed homes for professionals and entrepeneurs. Eckbo, whose national reputation was firmly established by the early 1940s, was immediately accepted as an equal by architects such as Ain and Quincy Jones. The idealistic mood of the post-war period resulted in several planned communities of which Mar

Richard Neutra, Lewin House, 1938. Curved bay window facing the Pacific Ocean with bluffs in background.

*Raphael Soriano, Shulman House, 1950. Garden
designed by Garrett Eckbo. The gravel path frames
cultivated gardens close to the house.*

Vista Housing (Gregory Ain, architect; 1948) and Crestwood Hills Mutual Housing (Whitney Smith and A. Quincy Jones, architects; 1947–51) are the most well known. Drawing on ideas that had grown out of low-cost housing proposals of the Depression era, these cooperative tracts were meant to appeal to returning war veterans and their families. They were designed for middle-income homeowners with children and no servants. The lots were compact and the houses opened at the rear to enclosed gardens or views. In these two large-scale projects, Eckbo's skills as a landscape architect were utilized to give the communities a unified identity. Using plant material—such as street trees at Mar Vista—to bridge the transition from private to public space, Eckbo demonstrated that the principles of modern landscape design could be transferred from the private garden to a more urban scale.

Eckbo's impact was most clearly felt, however, in the hundreds of private gardens that he designed for individual clients. He was skilled at addressing both the architectural elements of the modern house and the requirements of a rectangular suburban lot. By creating visual screens or boundaries with either plant material (hedges or rows of trees) or walls of industrial materials (aluminum or concrete block), Eckbo utilized dynamic forms to create dynamic spaces. By 1950, architectonic devices such as walls, fences, and hardscape dominated the horticulture, while pattern and texture were created with the use of pergolas and trellises as much as by plant material.

One thing is clear about the modernist garden in southern California: it was something more than a style. It represented a permanent shift from the traditional definition of a garden. Clients no longer came from royalty, they were families and professionals of the middle class; the houses were not palaces or grand estates on huge pieces of acreage, they were rectangular plots in a suburban context. These major social conditions, which still prevail, indicate that the principles of the modernist garden in southern California are as valid today as they were fifty years ago.

Endnotes

1 Bruce Kamerling, *Irving J. Gill, Architect,* (San Diego: San Diego Historical Society, 1993), 127.

2 Kamerling, *Irving J. Gill,* 126.

3 Frank Lloyd Wright, *An Autobiography* (New York: Duell, Sloan Pearce, 1943), 239.

4 Esther McCoy, *The Second Generation* (Salt Lake City, Utah: Gibbs M. Smith, Inc./Peregrine-Smith Books, 1984), 87.

First Modernist Garden: Rudolph M. Schindler—Clyde B. Chace House (1921-22)
Kathryn Smith

The southern California tradition of modern architecture with its roots in the principles and work of Irving Gill and Frank Lloyd Wright was advanced and expanded in the first independent design of Rudolph M. Schindler. The unexpected cessation of Wright's work in Los Angeles gave Schindler the opportunity to build his own studio-residence and open his own practice. In partnership with another couple—Clyde and Marian Chace—Schindler and his wife decided to build a cooperative dwelling that would contain three units: two L-shaped wings (housing studios for each individual), and a guest apartment. As radical as this social program was, Schindler's design was even more so.

Before Walter Gropius designed the Masters' Houses at the Bauhaus, before Le Corbusier built his first Citrohan house, and several years before Mies van der Rohe sketched out his plan for a brick country house, Schindler created a masterwork of continuous space that virtually erased the distinctions between inside and outside. It was 1921. Grounded in notions derived primarily from Wright, Schindler took the site as his point of departure thereby establishing one of the principal tenets of the southern California modernist garden. In this case, the site was a conventional rectangular suburban lot, 100 x 200 feet, surrounded on three sides by neighbors. Freed from the conventions of a typical house, Schindler conceived of each room as a universal space that opened to the gardens through sliding canvas doors and floor-to-ceiling glass screens. As a result, the building—a one-story pavilion placed low to the ground in the center of the site—has a pinwheel plan pivoting around a double fireplace. Rejecting symmetry as an organizing device, Schindler introduced visual axes, many of which are diagonal, which shift as the observer moves through the space.

With the entire site as his field, Schindler created a complex composition of horizontal and vertical spaces—some enclosed, most outdoors. Dispensing with the idea of a figure-ground relationship, he gave equal weight to the building and landscape. The strong horizontal planes of the house with flat roof and unfinished concrete floor (that continues as a surface into the garden as hardscape) modulate the horizontal flow of space toward the horizon. Except for perimeter walls around each studio, vertical planes of the building and in the garden overlap in space. The gardens were unprecedented: precise geometric planes creating a free plan. A work of modern art in nature.

It is clear that Schindler's garden was an expression of the changed social and economic circumstances of the modern era. Low-maintenance plants reflected the absence of servants, hedges and ground covers replaced floral splendor with textural and sculptural interest, and increased areas for recreation indicated new attitudes about healthy living for children and adults. During the 1920s, Richard Neutra and Schindler lived and worked side by side at the Schindler House. It was during this time that it attracted several young architects who would be profoundly influenced by the innovations they perceived in the plan: Ain, Harris, and Soriano. They would soon join Schindler and Neutra in southern California to create the most concentrated body of residential modern architecture in the world.

(Left) Interior of studio looking out to garden. Doorway frames view of heavenly bamboo.

(Opposite) When the sunken garden was restored, fountain grass (Pennisetum setaceum) was chosen where Schindler had just specified grass.

Rudolph M. Schindler— Clyde B. Chace House (1921–22)
Rudolph M. Schindler, architect

Despite the fact that the Schindler House was owned continuously by the family until it was acquired in 1980 by a non-profit organization, Friends of the Schindler House (FOSH), the gardens had retained little of their original plant material or form. Clearly, numerous plants had died, volunteers had sprung up in odd corners, and deferred maintenance had contributed to a feeling of an overgrown jungle. The mission of FOSH was to restore and conserve the Schindler House for future generations. As a result, a program was instituted in the 1980s by the director Robert Sweeney to return the gardens to the architect's original plan.

Sensitive interpretation was necessary throughout the restoration process since in most cases Schindler did not specify plants by name. One exception was his extensive use of Giant Bamboo (*Phyllostachys bambusoides*) as screen material; otherwise, his descriptions were general such as "hedge" or "high grass." Using historic photographs as a guide, choices were dependent on plants currently available that came closest to what Schindler had intended in the 1920s. Although the surrounding neighborhood was unbuilt at the time of construction—when the site was surrounded by farmland and a clear line of sight existed toward the Hollywood hills—Schindler had anticipated higher density. The plan called for visual protection from neighboring properties. Unfortunately, high-rise apartments currently hover overhead. The Schindler House is now used as an art exhibition space and is open to the public for tours of the building and gardens.

(Left) Outdoor fireplace viewed from second floor sleeping baskets.

(Bottom) Plot plan, 1921–22.

(Opposite) View past timber bamboo towards kitchen door.

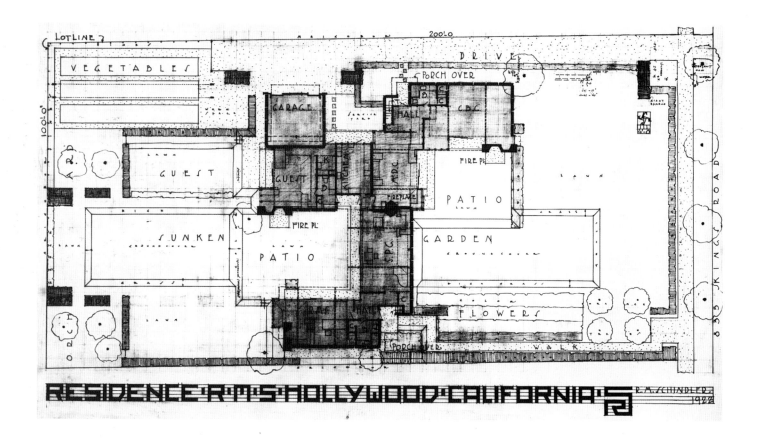

Richard J. Neutra and the Modernist Landscape in California

Pamela Burton and Richard Hertz

It was fifty years later when the southern California landscape architect Pamela Burton was presented with the opportunity to renew the gardens of several houses designed in the 1940s and 1950s by the modern architect Richard Neutra. The task of renewing a garden is clearly not the same as bringing it back to the state it was in when the house was just completed and the garden newly planted. The important question for Burton was "Just how much leeway should the designer have in 'adjusting' the original design to suit today's clients and needs?"

There are a variety of approaches that can be used when creating landscapes for these mid-century gardens. They include complete historical restoration, replacing exactly what was there at a specific year and date, and, at the opposite end of the spectrum, implementing a totally new design without keeping anything from the past. Strategies in-between these two approaches include adaptive re-use or modifying the original plans with new needs or functions re-interpreted in the garden; providing maintenance but letting everything stay as is; or just rehabilitating what exists. Burton's strategy was to work with the spirit of the plan by understanding the intentions of the architect while at the same time interpreting the client's current needs and incorporating them into the garden.

Understanding Neutra's intentions

Neutra had a number of general principles that governed the relationship of the house to its site. He valued the creation of serenity and privacy, "cooperating with the site," bringing the landscape into the home, and forming a "delightful fusion" of inside and outside. He also was adept at framing views in order to incorporate "borrowed landscapes," and creating illusions of space through the judicious use of plant materials.

However, Neutra was not a landscape architect and he did not look at landscape in the same way landscape architects do. It must be pointed out that Neutra served a brief, but important, apprenticeship in landscape before immigrating to the United States. In 1919, at the age of twenty-seven, Neutra worked in Otto Froebel's well-known Zurich nursery and landscape firm, under the tutelage of Gustav Ammann. During that time, his biographer Thomas S. Hines notes, he "developed an interest and facility in botany, landscaping,

and site planning that would serve him well the rest of his life."[1]

Although Neutra often indicated general instructions about how to achieve his goals, his later plans are remarkably free of references to specific plants and plant materials. Early in his career he made more detailed plans for gardens. In 1925, when he first moved to Los Angeles and he and his wife, Dione, lived with Rudolph and Pauline Schindler, he helped Schindler with specific landscape plans for two of Schindler's houses—the How House (1925) in Los Angeles and the Lovell House (1926) in Newport Beach. In these plans Neutra specified the sizes, types, and quantities of proposed plants. The garden spaces are laid out with low walls enclosing terraces and hedges forming the entry drive. His list includes pines, tamarix, erica, junipers, cotoneaster, acacias, eleagnus, eucalyptus, gazania, and honeysuckle. There are a number of other site plans for which he supervised the landscaping, and made specific botanical recommendations, for example, the Nesbitt House (1942) and the Lovell House designed for Los Angeles (1927–29).

Neutra's landscape plans for many other houses, however, were much more general in scope and detail. For example, in his plans for the Bald House (1941) in Ojai, he used a numbered key to show five types of landscape. His intention was to create a setting—a naturalistic, informal landscape to serve as a backdrop for his architecture and to diminish undesirable views. Number 2 keyed on his drawing shows "medium high shrubs which fall right up against the house, near the laundry room." In addition to the vague descriptions of massing materials, he often specified trees by using their botanical name. For example, at the Bald House he located and called for the *Acacia baileyana* tree. Although this tree does not exist there today, there is a similar bipinnate flowering tree (*Jacaranda acutifolia*) in approximately the same location.

Luxus—Intimacy and Liberation

In 1951, Neutra outlined his mature views about landscape in *Mystery and Realities of the Site*. He stated that all of our senses are affected by the setting: "It is one miraculous identity. What a site produces upon our total being is, in fact, a combined total impact—a magic spell, hard to gauge, to

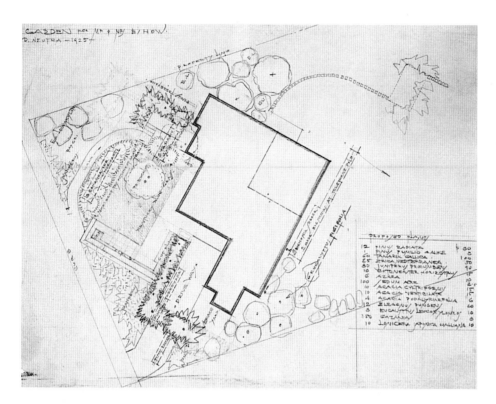

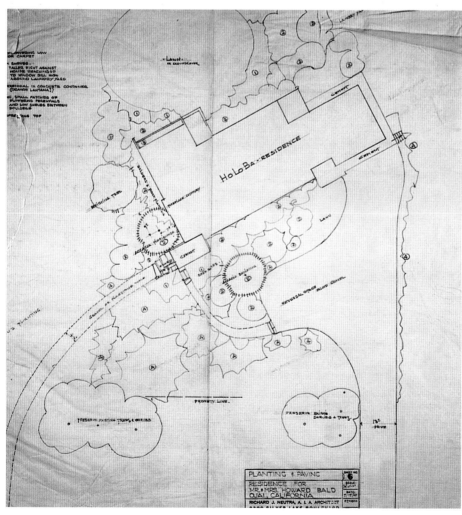

(Top) Richard Neutra for R.M. Schindler,
How House, landscape plan, 1925.

(Bottom) Richard Neutra, Bald House,
landscape plan, 1941.

(Opposite) Richard Neutra, Singleton House,
1959. View of Stone Canyon reservoir.

analyze or to exhaust in its effectiveness." It may seem surprising that a rigorous modernist architect such as Neutra, who focused upon the specificity of essential materials, forms, and structures, should have such seemingly mystical ideas about the relationship between people and landscape, house and site.

Historian Kenneth Frampton defined and explained an apparent paradox in Neutra's use of volumetric planes to enhance a "sense of luxus."[2] On the one hand, luxus is understood to imply "intimacy," and on the other hand, luxus implies the pleasure of "liberative space." Neutra's method of achieving spaces of both intimacy and liberation, Frampton concluded, hinged upon the presence of an invisible seam between inside and outside. Elements innovative at the time, such as sliding glass doors, outdoor and interior lighting, and the layering of horizontal planes functioned in unison to draw a transparent boundary between "our inner landscape of intimate organic effects" and the outer landscape of natural phenomena.[3] Describing the effect of an expanse of polished plate glass, Neutra wrote, "No corner post is needed, so the only visible division between indoors and out is the subtle sheen."[4] He continues, "Because the living room is separated from Nature only by the full-height thin-framed sliding doors of glass, the living space sweeps through and reaches out for miles until finally it is closed off by the mountain. The mountain is, indeed, the 'back wall' of this stupendous living room."[5]

intended. Where does the house end and the landscape begin? This fusion was one of Neutra's most important legacies.

Structural Tentacles and Pleasant Infiltration

His stress on horizontal layering and "movements down into the ground" (or site anchorage) exploited the horizontality of his houses and fused them with the landscape. This was accomplished through a series of parallel, echoing horizontal planes of pavement, roofline, ponds, pools, and contained planting rectangles. Adding to a sense of site anchorage are "structural tentacles," for example, walls and meandering walkways that extend from the house into the landscape to enfold some natural element within the surrounding site, thereby assuring rootedness in nature. And in reverse, the site is intertwined with the house by means of "pleasant infiltration," for example, an outdoor pool flowing into the house through a glass entry, or a stone patio continuing into the interior of the house. By bringing outdoor elements indoors as well as by "repeating nature's textures," home and site were fused both literally and metaphorically. Through the use of borrowed landscapes by the framing of distant vistas, the house became open to

Fusion of inside and outside

In the 1930s and 1940s, it was unusual to use lighting to create open and flowing space, joining inside and outside. Neutra was an innovator who used formal volumes in order to give spaces a "psychological, neurological meaning." He describes one of his rooms as "a fugue of classical peace in the midst of surrounding wilds." One framing device that Neutra used frequently in the post-war years was the "spider leg." He extended the silver painted fascia, which was attached to the roof edge, and brought it out six feet beyond the end of the house. This extension, which was held up by a thin, eight-foot spider leg of wood, served to elongate and give a greater sense of horizontal presence to the house. From the inside of the house looking out, the extended fascia and propping spider leg creates a permanent viewing device in which the inside and outside are fused as Neutra

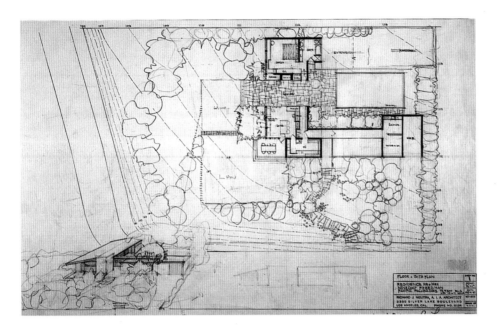

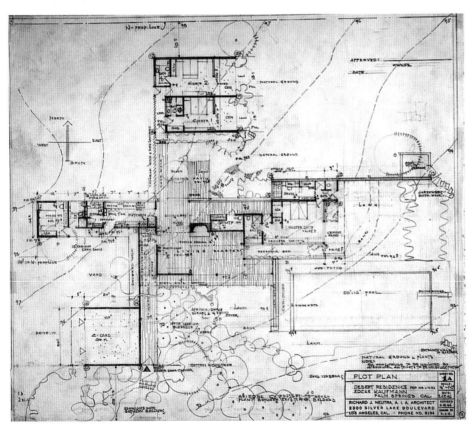

(Top) Richard Neutra, Freedman House, early landscape plan, 1947.

(Bottom) Richard Neutra, Kaufmann House, early landscape and grading plan, 1946.

the landscape. Indeed, the landscape directly around the house was often of less importance than the views beyond.

In his writings, Neutra instructs architects to look at the total environmental context of a site and consider what he called "the character and peculiarities of your site. Heighten and intensify what it may offer, never work against its inner grain and fiber."[6] The qualities of Neutra's houses—their space, openness, privacy, and sense of refuge—were integrally connected with their framing devices, their series of transposed horizontal planes, and the transparency of the house, so that the natural tapestry could be extended and fused into and through the volumetric architectural spaces.

Renewing Neutra's Gardens

An even deeper understanding of Neutra's intentions was gained after Burton completed gardens for two houses—Henry Singleton (1959) and Eugene Loring (1957–59). Her first commission was for the Singleton House, which became primarily an exercise in restoring the "borrowed landscape" that had distinguished this house originally. Since the garden had become badly overgrown over the decades, renewing the Singleton garden required skillful pruning to clarify the effects of time. Burton's primary responsibility for the Loring House was to reestablish the visual blending of inside and outside. To achieve this, she concentrated on the landscape immediately surrounding the house, allowing the idea of "tentacles" to re-emerge. But more importantly, her goal was to restore the distant views and "borrowed landscapes" originally established by Neutra's framing devices. The extended roofline was reflected in the rectangular pond below, while the "spider leg" framed an

idyllic view. By refurbishing the lawn at the top of the slope and placing indigenous stones between the pool and the view of the mountains, Burton restored the integrity of Neutra's composition.

The next garden that Burton was offered presented different challenges. Unlike the Singleton or Loring houses, the Benedict Freedman House (1947–49) in Pacific Palisades was built in a suburban neighborhood with houses flush to their lot lines. In the ensuing decades since the completion of the house, the site had lost privacy on both the street side and the side bordering the neighbor's property. Continuing Neutra's use of framing devices to extend the living space and create privacy, Burton examined the idea of containing the site with a combination of perimeter walls and fencing. Since the cul-de-sac street had now become a very popular gathering place to view the ocean, she created privacy by simplifying the entryway with stairs and a gate that echoed the horizontal lines of the house.

The Kaufmann House

According to Hines, the Edgar J. Kaufmann House (1946) in Palm Springs and the Burton Tremaine House in Montecito (1948) are the finest and most celebrated of Neutra's post-war houses. Neutra chose a pinwheel plan for the desert home to provide sweeping views in all directions. The gardens and surrounding landscape on the generous 200 x 300-foot lot were a result of circumstance and time. In order to take advantage of the spectacular site, but at the same time provide privacy for the family, Neutra planned a screening hedge to be planted along the road between existing boulders. Subsequently, he prepared an elaborate

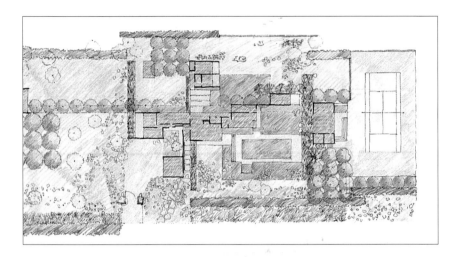

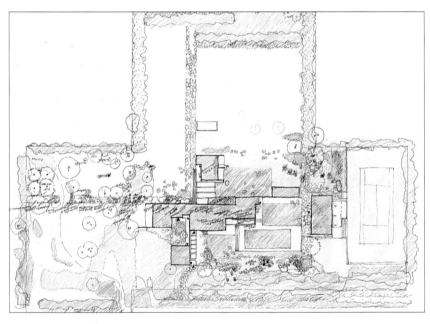

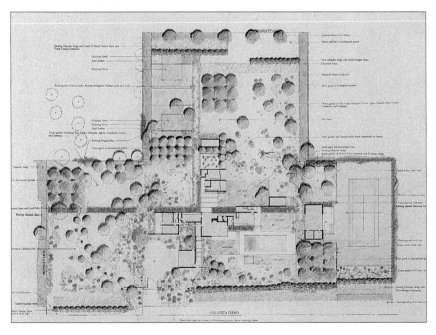

(Top) Pamela Burton & Company, Kaufmann House, landscape plan, 1994.

(Middle) Pamela Burton & Company, Kaufmann House, landscape plan after additional property was acquired, 1994.

(Bottom) Pamela Burton & Company, Kaufmann House, landscape sketch, 1994.

*Pamela Burton & Company, Kaufmann House,
site model, 1994.*

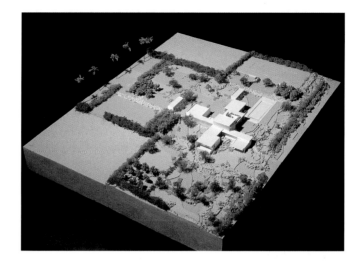

plant list of ten pages, "Suggestions for Fall Plantings, 1946," of which some of the larger specimens remain on the property today. He divided the land into distinct zones; for example, Area C is called a Morning Rest Area and Area A is the northeasterly property line screening. Mrs. Kaufmann also had a list of plant materials, for example, camellias and roses, all of which could either freeze or fry in the desert.

After the initial installation, the Kaufmanns moved in, and became friends with Patricia Moortens and her husband, known by all as Cactus Slim. The Moortens took them to Joshua Tree National Monument in order to show them the beauty of the desert flora. As a result of this friendship, the Kaufmanns introduced more native plants into their immediate surroundings, thereby modifying Neutra's original intentions.

When the current owners purchased the house, the open desert had given way to increasing population. To begin restoration, they purchased lots to the north, west, and east (essentially tripling the size of the site) reestablishing the feeling of expansive space. Pamela Burton was asked to make a new landscape design for the enlarged property. Goals were set to unify the larger site, screen out the encroaching suburbia, and regain the borrowed landscape. The second strategy was to give the cultivated landscape the same rigor as the house and to invite the wild desert back in to recreate what Neutra described as "the lightness of a ship on the sand." This was accomplished by tailoring the lawn into discrete green rectangles adjacent to usable spaces of the house. The pinwheel plan was mirrored in the landscape with a red stripe of plant materials, comprised of red

pennisetum, burgundy coral bells, red lobelia, and dwarf hop bush, with a red Indian sandstone walking surface. The stones inside these bands were both native boulders as well as pavers interplanted with native grasses. The overall effect was intended to create subtle lines that extend from the house, disappear, and reappear again. Subsequently, this plan was not implemented and the drawings remain as a record of the design process.

Gardens are ephemeral. The act of renewing them poses unique problems for both the homeowner and the landscape architect. The gardens of mid-century modern houses are even more difficult because they are still close enough to us in time that they do not appear historical, yet their design can be crucial to experiencing the original intentions of the architect. However, with greater understanding of such fundamental principles as the fusion of the inside and outside, the duality of structural tentacles and pleasant infiltration, and the creation of a sense of luxus, the designer can reinterpret a client's contemporary needs with greater sensitivity.

Endnotes

1 Thomas S. Hines, *Richard Neutra and the Search for Modern Architecture* (New York: Oxford University Press, 1982), 26.

2 Kenneth Frampton's remarks appear in an untitled video interview that was conducted in 1995 by Elizabeth Harris and Ron Radziner.

3 Kenneth Frampton in untitled video interview with Harris and Radziner.

4 Richard Neutra, *Mystery and Realities of the Site* (Scarsdale, New York: Morgan and Morgan, 1951), 27.

5 *Mystery*, 24

6 *Mystery*, 62.

Mid-Century Gardens: Richard J. Neutra

Pamela Burton and Marie Botnick

Albert Lewin House (1938)

Howard Bald House (1941)

John B. Nesbitt House (1942)

Benedict Freedman House (1947)

Warren Tremaine House (1947–48)

Henry Singleton House (1959)

More than any other southern California architect of his generation, Richard Neutra enjoyed an international reputation during his lifetime. In 1932, with only one major building completed—the Lovell House—he was included in the landmark show, "International Exhibition of Modern Architecture," at the Museum of Modern Art in New York City. Seventeen years later, in 1949, he was on the cover of *Time* magazine, hailed as one of the most influential modern architects in the world. Despite this level of acclaim, Neutra was best known not for monumental public buildings, but for houses, and small suburban houses for the middle class, at that. It is important to point out that after World War II, he was offered several commissions from clients with greater resources—Edgar Kaufmann and Warren Tremaine, especially—that gave him an opportunity to extend and develop his ideas on a larger scale.

The evolution of the small house in Neutra's work is striking, but not especially noteworthy for his skill with elements such as structural innovation, spatial complexity, or refinements in plan. Rather it is notable for the ingenious way that the architect utilized technical advances in glass manufacture to deepen the relationship of the interior of the house to the out-of-doors. A clear distinction exists between the work before and after World War II when large sheets of plate glass became readily available. In the earlier houses such as the Albert Lewin House (1938), Neutra uses bands of windows of uniform height and width across the face of the wall. In the houses after the war, such as the Eugene Loring House (1957–59) or the Henry Singleton House (1959), Neutra eliminated steel casement windows in favor of composing the wall of simple planes—alternating transparent screens of floor-to-ceiling glass with solid walls of concrete or wood. Through the vast expanses of glass walls, Neutra invited the landscape into the interior as a welcome element while, at the same time, he extended the living space of the small house to the horizon.

Albert Lewin House (1938)
Richard J. Neutra, architect

Designing for film producer-director Albert Lewin, Richard Neutra created a luxurious environment for entertaining Hollywood's literati. Built on a narrow 50 foot x 200-foot lot facing Santa Monica Bay, the house and landscaped courts extended to the property line. The most distinguished feature of the house is the curve of the living room that faces out to the bay.

The present owners enlarged the property by purchasing an adjoining 50 x 200-foot lot to the south and hired Steven Ehrlich to design an entertainment pavilion and a swimming pool. Ehrlich sought to integrate his design with Neutra's by utilizing a similar approach to site design and appropriating the curve of the living room to become the cross-section of the pavilion roof. To make the grade transition between the original and the new lot, landscape architect Barry Beer created elongated concrete steps with planted treads leading from the new pool down to the existing garden. The planted steps are part of a linear garden that serves as a transition between the old and the new. The two elements that Beer used in this linear garden are lawn and *Festuca mairei* (Moroccan fescue) grasses.

A central axis directs the view out through floor-to-ceiling glass toward both the bay and the sky. Ehrlich solved the privacy problem by designing an ingenious sliding wall that alternately opens and closes the pool and garden to the beautiful white sand beach and expansive ocean view. The pavilion opens on the east to a courtyard that is bounded by the Neutra house, the new garage, and concrete posts and beams. This garden court is composed of two basic elements of lawn and bamboo, discreetly placed in a planting bed created as a niche in the wall of the garage.

In a minimalist composition that promotes serenity in the garden, Beer used a limited palette of plant materials including grasses, a low ligustrum hedge, bamboo, and Queen palm trees. An allée of fourteen podacarpus trees was planted along the pavilion for privacy, to screen the adjacent neighbor's house. He also used shade-tolerant plants such as white camellias with vinca ground cover. A cluster of black bamboo dramatically offsets the view from inside the vaulted structure. By consistently using the same grasses throughout, Beer has fused the inside with the outside. Upon entering, the contrast from a busy street to the calm of the garden is dramatic.

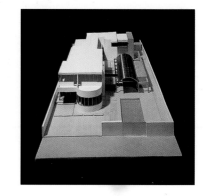

(Right) Steven Ehrlich, Model of original house with addition, 1996.

Original Plat Plan

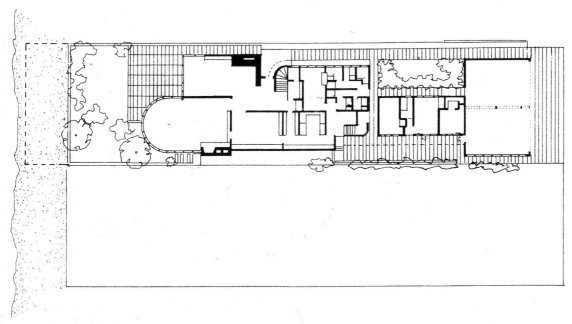

Contemporary Plot Plan

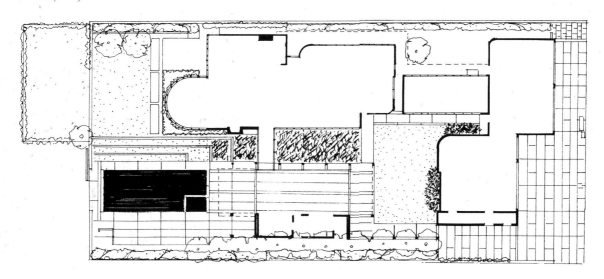

(Above) Entryway garden with rectangular stepping stones planted with tropicals such as Dieffenbachia and ginger, c. 1930s.

(Opposite, top) View of entertainment pavilion from second floor.

(Opposite, bottom left) Swimming pool with sliding wall open to white sand beach.

(Opposite, bottom right) View of pavilion from pool looking back to palm-studded Santa Monica bluff.

(Top) Linear concrete steps down to lawn. Bay window base planted with privet hedge.

(Bottom) Interior of pavilion looking out to garden court planted with bamboo and grasses.

Howard Bald House (1941)

Richard J. Neutra, architect

On a broad two-acre site with a view of the Ojai Valley, Richard Neutra designed the house of a psychiatrist and his wife. Although the property was surrounded by orange groves, Neutra placed the house so that views of the valley could be maintained from most of the rooms. The approach from the street descends into a motor court. The rectangular plan is organized with a corridor dividing the kitchen and dining room on one side from the living room, study, and bedroom on the other. Both sides of the house are banded with glass so that the kitchen and dining room look out over a low row of guavas and junipers to the Topa Topa Mountains. The living room takes full advantage of the site to gain a spectacular 180-degree view of the entire Ojai Valley through a corner of glass and a screened porch.

In a drawing dated May 15, 1941 Neutra specified plant materials according to a list of categories with a numbered key as follows: Perennials, a low carpet of color; medium high shrubs taller against the house reaching up near the laundry; flowering perennials for the concrete planters (orange lantana); rock planting, small patches and low shrubs between boulders; and a tree with a spreading top. The tree was specified as an acacia and has since been replaced with a jacaranda. The present owners are avid gardeners and have created a garden consisting of a lawn terrace and a viewing meadow below the living room, with the use of plants such as buckwheat, Manzanita, Matilija and California poppies.

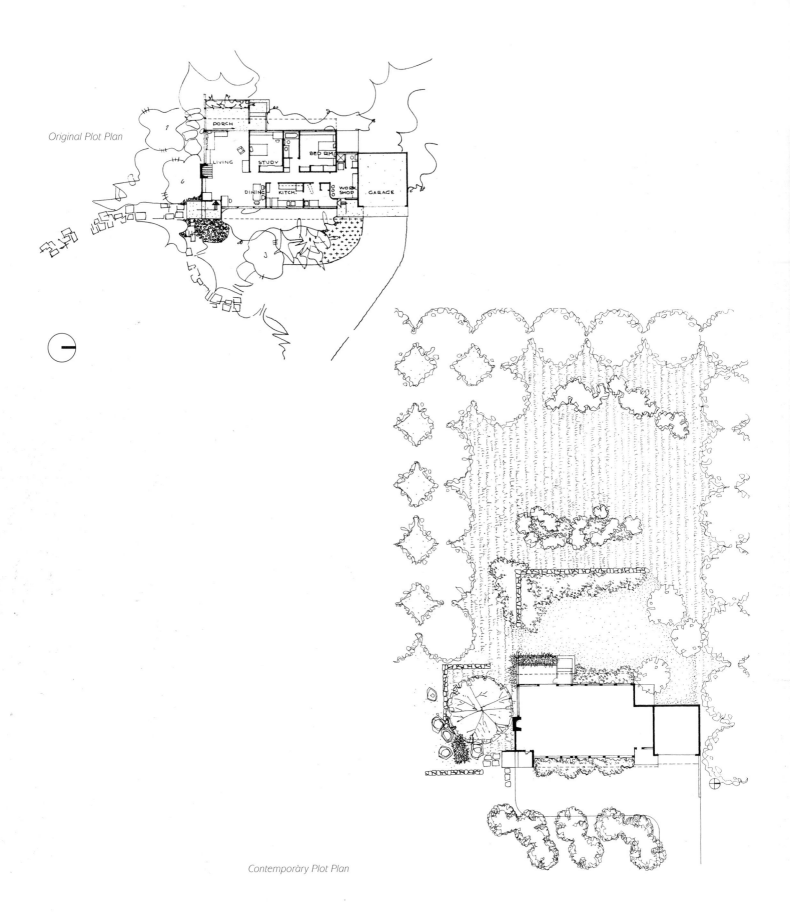

Original Plot Plan

PORCH

LIVING

STUDY

BED RM.

DINING

KITCH.

WORK SHOP

GARAGE

Contemporàry Plot Plan

40

(Above) Site before planting. c. 1940s.

(Top) View of house with rose garden, embraced by live oak and jacaranda trees.

(Bottom) Path leading to screen porch with distant view of Topa Topa Mountain Range.

(Top) Original live oak tree frames house.

(Bottom) Screen porch with walk lined with agapanthus and bearded iris.

43

John B. Nesbitt House (1942)
Richard J. Neutra, architect

Building for NBC radio producer John B. Nesbitt in Brentwood, an exclusive neighborhood in West Los Angeles, Neutra placed the house at the center of the spacious flat site to create both a front and rear garden. A diagonal walk brings the visitor into an entry veranda with a lily pond that continues under the glass door into the foyer. Built of redwood and glass, the house is comprised of two linear wings that are connected by a breezeway with all rooms opening to the gardens through sliding glass doors.

The present owner, a dedicated gardener, hired landscape architect Thomas Cox to help realize her vision for a tropical garden. The diagonal walk was framed with masses of king palms and Australian tree ferns. Rare and exotic ginger was grouped in screens to direct the views out from the bedroom wing toward a rill that flows into a reflecting pool. Some of the original circular ponds were eliminated, while others were added. Running parallel to the breezeway, Neutra's brick serpentine wall was replanted with a flowering border including scented nutmeg, peppermint geraniums, sorrel, agapanthus, azaleas, and camellias. The views from the living room out towards the swimming pool were framed by masses of bananas and Australian tree ferns. Plants introduced in mass include King palms (*Archontophoenix cunninghamiana*), Australia tree ferns (*Dicksonia antarctica*), Giant Bird of Paradise (*Strelitzia nicolai*), ginger (*Hedycium zingiberaceae*), jasmine, and heliconia.

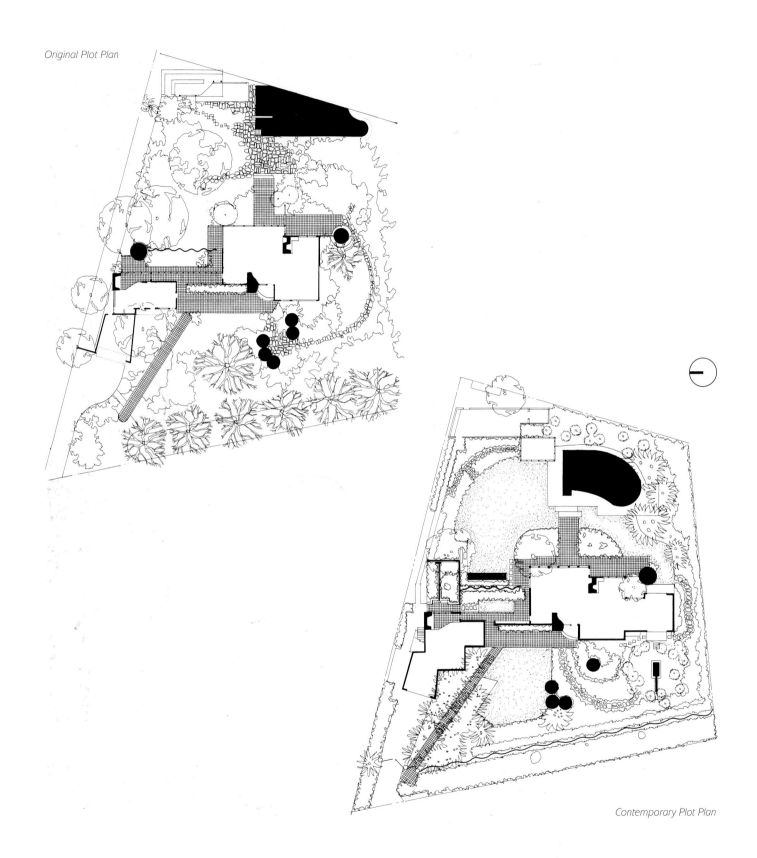

Original Plot Plan

Contemporary Plot Plan

46

(Top) Indoor-outdoor lily pond with intersecting sliding glass door, c. 1940s.

(Bottom) Brick serpentine wall encloses garden, c. 1940s.

(Overleaf) Living room with sliding door open to brick patio and garden, mid 1950s.

(Opposite) New planting of king palms along original diagonal brick walk.

(Left) Herb garden at base of serpentine wall includes sorrel, scented geraniums, rehmannia, and azaleas.

(Below) Metal dish recessed into ground cover with elephant ears and kentia palm.

(Opposite) Rectangular pond with rill and tree fern.

(Above) Spider leg extending towards swimming pool deck.

Benedict Freedman House (1947–49)
Richard J. Neutra, architect

This ocean bluff house in Pacific Palisades was designed for Benedict Freedman, a comedy writer for Jack Benny, Bob Hope, and Red Skelton. Surrounding the property are majestic blue gum eucalyptus as old as the house. The L-shaped plan wraps around a landscaped court with a swimming pool. A clear line of sight extends dramatically from the end of the pool through floor-to-ceiling glass doors across the living room to the garden and a view of the Pacific Ocean beyond. Neutra's original plant selection consisted of acacia, deodar cedar, Algerian ivy, *Pittosporum tobira, Agave attenuata,* and a Cup-of-Gold vine trained on redwood trusses that were suspended over the swimming pool.

The new owners, Bruce and Marie Botnick, worked closely with Peter Grueneisen of Studio Baüton and Pamela Burton & Company to create a pleasing sensation of continuous space through the use of carefully manipulated landscape elements. A defined lawn area was added on the south to establish an architectural extension in the landscape and to frame views of the ocean. A meandering path connects the garden shed to a viewing platform on a lower level. The design includes a series of simple, plaster walls and a gate in keeping with the horizontal planes of the house. They step up the slope from the street to the front entry. Marie Botnick designed a low, rectangular fishpond planted with water lilies and elephant's ear (*Colocasia esculenta*). A sequence of outdoor rooms wrap around the kitchen wing on the east side including a dining terrace, vegetable garden, and a garden shed.

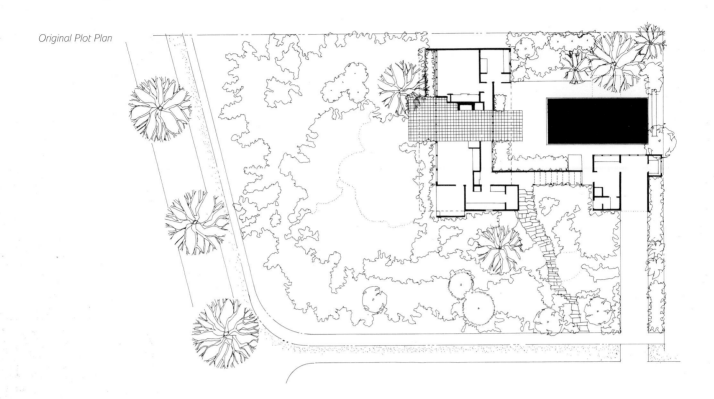
Original Plot Plan

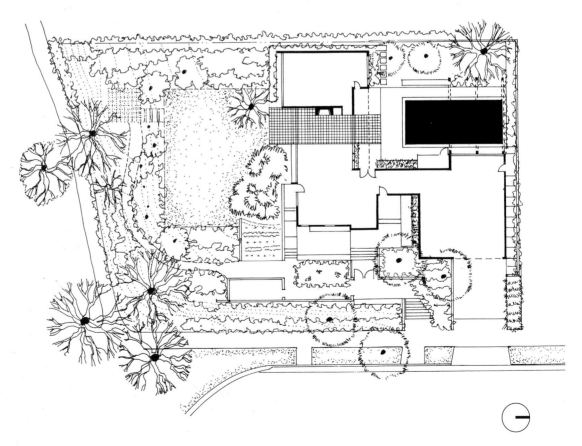
Contemporary Plot Plan

(Above) Benedict and Nancy Freedman with family on tiled patio overlooking ocean bluff, c. 1950s.

(Right) Redwood trellis covered with Copa de Oro vine designed to screen neighbor's roof, c. 1950s.

(Previous spread) New front entry steps and stucco walls. Hillside planted with Ceanothus *and accented with blue agave and opuntia.*

(Above) Terraced vegetable garden with potted succulent lies adjacent to the potting shed. Westringia rosmariniformis, Echium fastuosum, Agave attenuata, Opuntia *and* Leptospermum lavigatum *grow along decomposed granite path, which leads to ocean viewing patio.*

(Opposite) Elephant ears accent a rectangular fish pond with tropical water lilies and rare Cape Reed grass.

(Above) Living and dining room viewed through corner glass, plumeria tree, and original grouping of Agave attenuata.

(Overleaf) Two butterfly chairs on ocean-front lawn with echium, Leptospernum lavigateum, *flax, helichrysum, and lavender planted on hillside.*

Warren Tremaine House (1947–48)

Richard J. Neutra, architect

On sixteen acres of undulating meadow with California
sycamores and coast live oaks, Neutra designed one of his
most important houses. In the foothills of Santa Barbara, the
pinwheel plan of the house takes advantage of distant views
of the mountains while cultivating living spaces outdoors with
radiant-heated terrazzo floors. Perhaps Siegfried Giedion, the
architectural critic, gave the best description in a letter to
Neutra in 1950, "Your Tremaine House still is vividly in my
mind. There the right of matter, man's freedom of movement,
and the affinity to the organic surroundings are welded into a
unity by deepest penetration into the constructive possibilities
of expression. One detail showed that for me more
impressively than anything else; the view out of the master
bedroom onto the microcosm of tree trunks and rocks, left
admirably in their placidity by the architect."

Initially, Neutra worked with Lockwood de Forest in grading
the site and planting an informal mix of flowers and annuals
among the boulders. Neutra writes in *Mystery and Realities
of the Site*, "Large boulders, dug out during excavation and
piled against the terrace slope, and the adjoining wall,
instead of being carted away, become sculptural forms that
soon are softly coated with moss and lichens."

After Lockwood de Forest died in 1949, Ralph Stevens
designed a low maintenance garden primarily of succulents
off the living-dining terrace. This display was modulated at
the ground plane by blue senecio and mossy Korean grass
(*Xyosia tenuifolia*). Extending out from the living room is the
west terrace, which reaches into the garden between two
microclimates separating the heat of the succulents and the
coolness of the fern garden. In 1950, Katherine Tremaine
wrote Neutra to answer his letter in which he stated that the
ferns were not compatible with the oaks, "... We are
delighted to see the tree ferns, even though, as you say, they
do not belong to the same environment. To us the filtered
sunlight playing on the delicate fronds and the moss below
is a charming sight and gives one a pleasing psychological
feeling ... in striking contrast to the succulents in the bright
sun on the opposite side of the loggia."

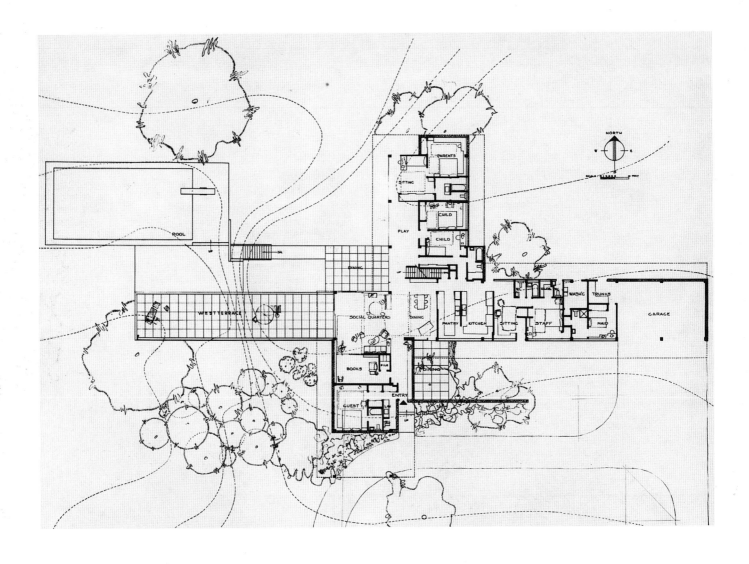

(Above) Master bedroom wing with mitred glass window is carefully inserted into the earth without disturbing existing oaks, before 1949.

(Overleaf) Large boulders gathered from the grading of the site were used as sculptural supports for the garden banks, before 1949.

(Above) View of house from radiant heated bridge terrace, after 1949.

(Opposite) Early photo of succulent garden, after 1949.

West facing bank planted with succulents designed by Ralph Stevens, after 1949. His overall concept was to use the structural, fleshy, smooth foliage of aloe, agave, and dracenas in contrast to the colorful low-growing crassulas, echeverias, and aeoniums.

(Above) View to cool fern dell through breezeway, 1980s.

(Opposite) Along stone path, fern dell is planted with Kentia palm, Australian tree ferns, baby tear moss and agapanthus.

Henry Singleton House (1959)

Richard J. Neutra, architect

In order to take full advantage of the spectacular property off Mulholland Drive, Richard Neutra sited the house for Henry Singleton, co-founder of Teledyne Incorporated, at the crest of the ridge with sweeping views of the Stone Canyon reservoir. After ascending into the motor court, a stepped walk leads up to the entry with a wood pergola overhead. Neutra used the boulders recovered from grading the pad to retain the slope and frame the stairs. The cruciform plan creates L-shaped spaces that define gardens. The most dramatic area of the garden is framed by a spider leg. Through a mitred corner glass window of the living room, the visitor can look out above a reflecting pool to the water of the Stone Canyon reservoir in the distance. Neutra's use of borrowed landscape as well as the reflective qualities of the water and the glass are uniquely woven together to create a depth of perception that surpasses much of his other work.

Pamela Burton worked with Rolla Wilhite to clear the site and, using existing pine trees, framed the restored views of the reservoir.

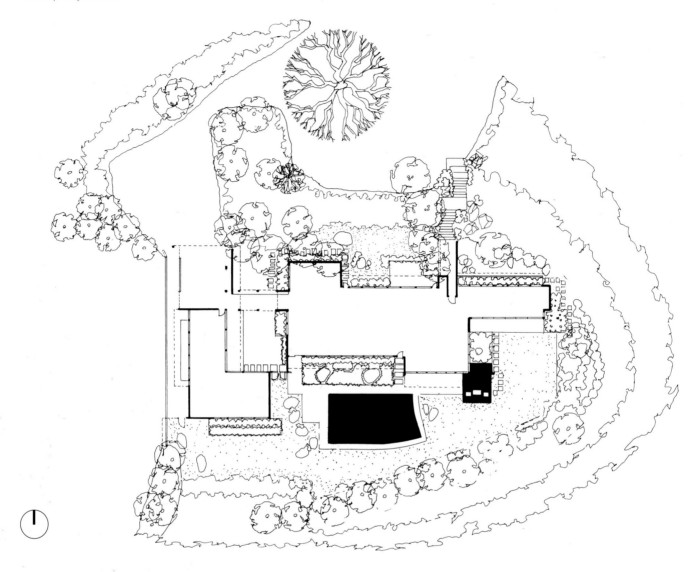

(Above) View towards house and reflecting
pond, c. 1960s.

(Right) Night view, c. 1960s.

(Opposite) Entry to front door under the canopy of several multi-trunk Brazilian pepper trees bordered with ferns, iris, and philodendron.

(Above) South elevation of living room with spider leg composition and plantings of cycad and ferns. Aleppo pines hover in background.

(Above) *View of reservoir through mitred glass.*

(Above) Composition of spider leg, mitred glass, and reflecting pond.

(Overleaf) View of house and swimming pool.

Mid-Century Gardens:

Pamela Burton and
Marie Botnick

Willard Hall Francis, Willard Hall Francis House (1934–35)

R.M. Schindler, C.C. Fitzpatrick House (1936)

Harwell Hamilton Harris, Dean McHenry House (1940)

J.R. Davidson, James Vigeveno House (1941)

Raphael Soriano, Richard Strauss House (1941)

J.R. Davidson, Jack Shapiro House (1943/1948–49)

Gregory Ain, Mar Vista Housing (1946–48)

A. Quincy Jones, Robert Haas House (1948)

Raphael Soriano, Julius Shulman House (1950)

Joseph van der Kar, Albert Wohlstetter House (1953)

A. Quincy Jones, Jones-Emmons Office (1954)

A. Quincy Jones & Frederick E. Emmons, Gary Cooper House (1961)

John Lautner, Sheats-Goldstein House (1963)

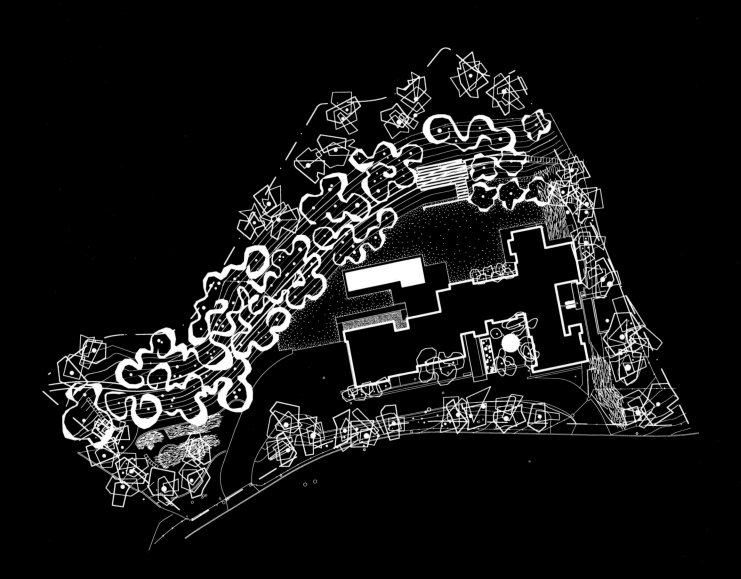

In the early decades of the twentieth century, the ideals of modern architecture were clearly defined by Le Corbusier's visionary plan for an urban utopia. The Radiant City, as it was known, was originally designed as a replacement for world-weary capitals of Europe such as Paris, Berlin and Rome which European modernists regarded as unhealthy, congested, and alienating. Instead Le Corbusier believed that modernism aspired to the three essential joys of living: sun, space, and greenery. Perhaps one of the greatest ironies of modern architecture is the fact that the ideals of "The Radiant City" were never realized on a large scale in Europe, but rather in southern California in a form that Le Corbusier would never have recognized.

It was here that all the necessary ingredients came together: a region free from paralyzing traditions, a terrain that offered varied building opportunities, a balmy climate of warm winters and dry summers, and an abundant supply of imported water. These were the elements that were available to a generation of architects that included Harwell Hamilton Harris, Raphael Soriano, Gregory Ain, Joseph van de Kar, and A. Quincy Jones among others. Surprisingly free of theoretical trappings, by the early 1960s, these young architects created the largest concentration of modern houses in the world. These mid-century modern houses were primarily one-story in height with flat roofs, sliding glass doors, and living spaces that flowed into gardens. With abundant areas of glass they epitomized Le Corbusier's essential joys of modern living: sun, space, and greenery.

Willard Hall Francis House (1935)
Willard Hall Francis, architect

Willard Hall Francis, inspired by Frank Lloyd Wright, designed and built this house for himself and his wife. Sited on the edge of a hill surrounded by the Topa Topa mountains to the north, the house opens up through mitred-glass corner windows to a splendid view of the verdant Ojai Valley. The entry drive to the west wraps around a planter containing an exotic array of agaves, *Aloe arborescens,* opuntia cacti, and a rare bromeliad (*Puya berteroniana*). Steps lead down from the driveway to the entrance which is protected overhead with a wood trellis intertwined with purple wisteria. The architect took advantage of the sloping terrain by building retaining walls of Ojai rock that framed outdoor spaces and extended the horizontality of the roof plane. Gravel paths planted with lavender, rosemary, and other drought-tolerant plants wind through the garden. Eucalyptus, acacia, and several tea trees (*Leptospermum laevigatum*) provide strong accents. The house and garden are seamlessly integrated through the use of consistent materials: native stone for walls and painted wood for trim, trellises, and railings.

(Opposite) Willard Hall Francis stands under wood trellis at front entrance of his house in Ojai, c. 1935–40. Newly planted wisteria vine climbs the pergola.

(Right) House is sited with backdrop of Topa Topa mountain range, c. 1935–40.

(Below) Aerial view of house showing entry drive and arroyo with native chaparral to the left, c. 1935–40.

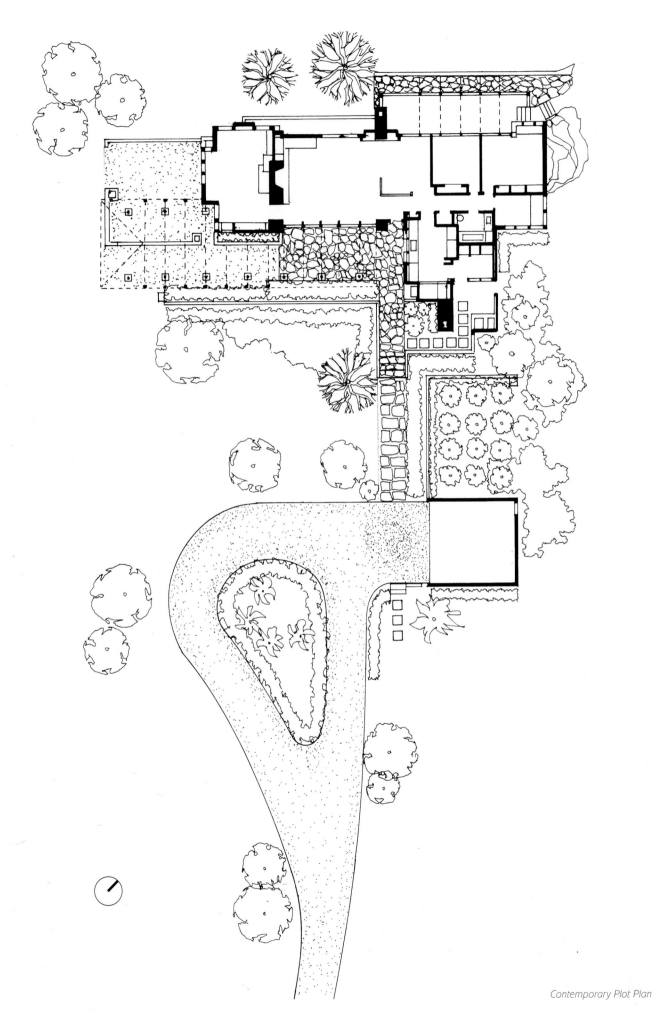

Contemporary Plot Plan

(Right) West elevation of house with view of Ojai Valley in the distance, c. 1935–40.

(Bottom) Driveway with the central cactus garden, c. 1935–40.

(Opposite) View of house from garden below.

(Above) Garden stone walk leads to front entry with live oak canopys.

(Top) Trellis and rock garden.

(Above) Central cactus garden with oak tree.

(Top, left) Opuntia cactus with rare bromeliad
(Puya berteroniana).

(Middle, right) Agave villnoreaneama.

(Above, right) Detail of Puya Bromeliad in bloom.

(Opposite) Entrance to house and garden paved
with Ojai rock; pergola entwined with Japanese
wisteria vine.

(Right) House and garden offset with gravel paths winding through plantings of lavender, rosemary, and succulents.

C.C. Fitzpatrick House (1936)
R.M. Schindler, architect

In his landmark study, *Schindler*, the architectural historian David Gebhard writes of the C.C. Fitzpatrick House that it "was meant to be theatrical." It was built, he explains, "as a come-on for new speculative land development at the top of the Hollywood hills." Its intimacies, however, are nested in privacy.

Russ Leland, who bought the property in the early 1990's, found an oval swimming pool, added by previous owners in the 1960's, bordered with roses, geraniums, and bougainvillaea. Because these plantings interfered with the clean lines of the house, Leland and landscape designer Jay Griffith replaced them with flax, westringia, succulents, and fortnight lilies. They used concrete pavers for decking and benches in an imaginative fashion, surrounding them with these ornamental plants. For the challenge and whimsy of it, an outdoor shower was placed on a flagstone terrace below the house. Shielded from view, it can be used at any hour, and especially at night under the stars. The addition of a chicken coop brings a rural charm to the garden, to the delight of the owners.

This garden epitomizes Garrett Eckbo's phrase, "Gardens can be homes of delight, of fantasy, of imagination, of adventure, as well as of relaxation and repose."

(Above) Expansive lawn offsets the strong horizontality of the structure, c. 1930s.

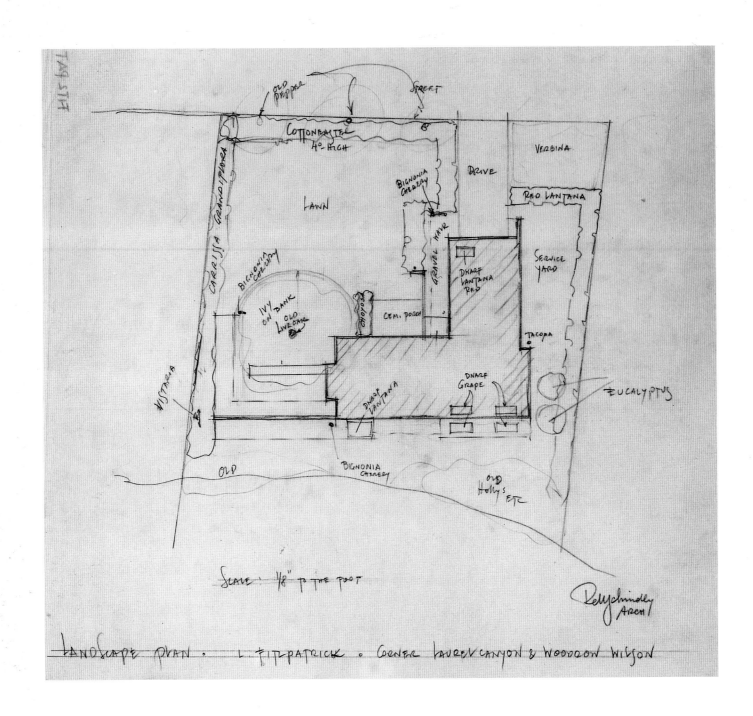

(Above) R.M. Schindler, Landscape Plan, c. 1936.

(Above) Concrete bench with poured concrete pavers set in artemesia, ornamental grasses, lavender, fortnight lilies, and potted succulents.

(Right) Outdoor shower on the lower flagstone patio with outdoor kitchen.

(Far right) One-of-a-kind concrete garden pots cast by the homeowner.

(Left) Round swimming pool mirrors the Mediterranean plantings of lavender, ornamental grasses, fortnight lilies, flax, and succulents. Geometric configuration of concrete pavers edged with lawn.

(Below) Chicken coop set alongside swimming pool.

(Left) Outdoor living room with fireplace and wood storage.

(Opposite) Rectangular stepping stones set in Mexican pebbles lead to stairs of new entry.

Dean McHenry House (1940)
Harwell Hamilton Harris, architect

Several years ago, Brian Tichenor and Raun Thorp of Tichenor & Thorp, Architects, purchased the one-story house and through Brian's aunt's association with the Dean McHenry family, they were able to acquire the original house plans. The husband and wife team has used the house and garden as a laboratory for exploring ideas about landscape and architecture. The site, approximately one third of an acre, in West Los Angeles, is divided into three levels; the street level at which the garage and original entry to the house is located; the main level, at which the house is located; and the pool level, which is up a set of stairs flanked on either side by potted succulents and cacti.

Harwell Hamilton Harris's original cruciform plan created four distinct outdoor courts, in addition to the upper pool garden. Dramatically, every room opens onto a garden, patio or water feature. The living room and kitchen share a patio with an outdoor fireplace. the courtyard off the kitchen functions as a children's play area. On one side of the master bedroom a garden court connects to the studio/guesthouse and on the other, a Japanese garden with a water lily pond. Plant material used in the Japanese garden includes: *Acer palmatum atropurpureum*, "bloodgood" (Japanese Maple), *Anigozanthos* "Big Red", *Nandinadomestica* "Nana", *Abutilon vesuvius*, Liriope, and *Berberis thunbergiii* "Royal Burgundy". The new entry court is comprised of Mexican river-washed pebbles with rectangular stepping stones that pass through an undulating hedge of *Westringea rosmariniformis*, *Dodonea* and *Eriobotrya* "Coppertone". The largest space is devoted to the swimming pool with its own cabana/teahouse which is bordered by a lily pond with an urn-fountain. Mature trees and hedges of *Westringea rosmariniformis*, Bronze Banana, *Anigozanthos flavidus*, *Dodonea viscosa* "Purpurea", *Phormium tenax*, *Trachelium caerleum*, and water lilies surround the pool area.

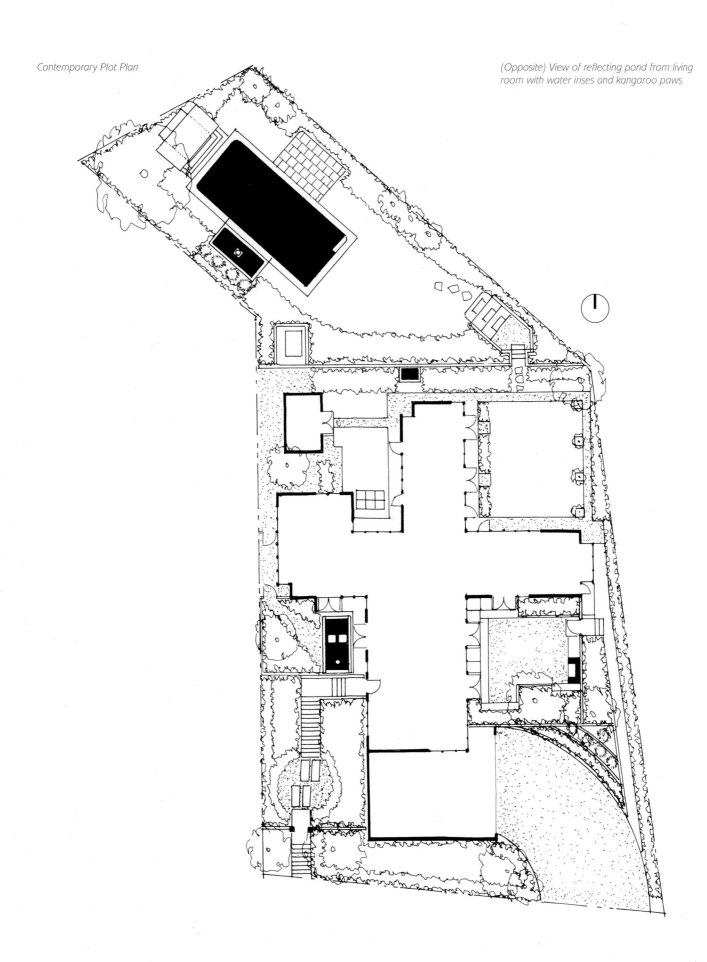

Contemporary Plot Plan

(Opposite) View of reflecting pond from living room with water irises and kangaroo paws.

(Above, left) Koi pond with urn fountain adjacent
to the swimming pool, with plantings of
Dondonea viscosa 'Purpurea', Phormium tenax,
Geranium incanum, and waterlily.

(Above, right) Stairs up to pool flanked by cereus
cactus potted succulents and flax in urns.

(Above, left) View toward house from pool with
flax 'Maori Chief', Euphorbia characias,
kangaroo paw, Aeonium, and agave.

(Above, right) Reflecting pond in Japanese
garden with wisteria trailing bamboo fence.

(Left) Pool and teahouse/cabaña.

(Above) Courtyard with large urns.

(Left) Early photo of entry court with oak, c. 1940s.

James Vigeveno House (1941)

J.R. Davidson, architect

Originally built as a vacation retreat for a Los Angeles art dealer, this Ojai house is perched on a gently sloping two-acre hilltop, protected by oaks (*Quercus agrifolia*) and lemon gums (*Eucalyptus citriodora*). The north side of the house has a sitting porch with a view of the mountains, while a second larger porch for dining off the living room looks over the Ojai Valley. The current owners Rick and Eva Rossovich, undertook a remodeling that expanded the kitchen and created a new entry. The present garden focuses on three major areas. When the former kitchen garden was enclosed to enlarge the kitchen, a new garden planter and wall were constructed to direct visitors to the front door. Elaborate gardens were terraced on the slope to replace bare-raked earth. They were planted with drought-tolerant, bold, graphic materials such *Agave americana, Aloe thraskii,* sedums, crassulas, other aloes, and senecios. Additional gardens were planted between a swimming pool built in the late 1940s and a pool house added by the current owners to serve as an art and yoga studio. Drought-tolerant plants chosen were draecenas, aeoniums, artemesia, echiums, and various succulents.

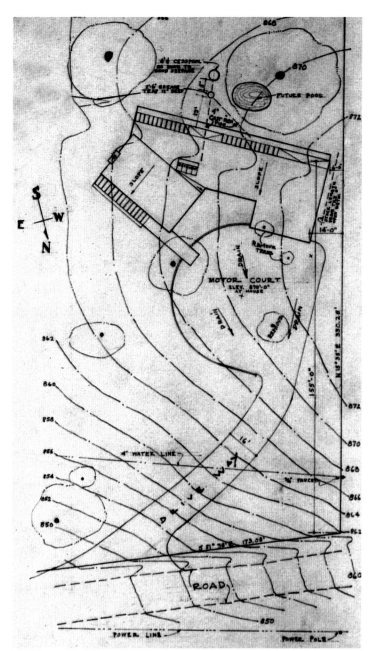

(Left) Original Plot Plan

(Below) Original House Plan

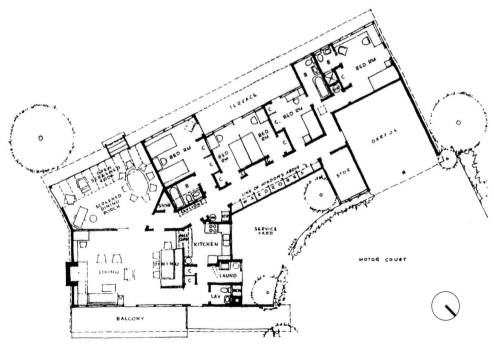

115

(Above) View of private landscape with oaks, c. 1940s.

(Left) East elevation showing screen with views of the valley, c. 1940s.

(Above) View of Ojai Valley through screened porch.

(Right) North elevation.

(Above) New entry to house with plaster walls planted with Aloe arborescens.

(Above) Kitchen garden planted with succulents under oaks.

(Left) Agave ferox *underplanted with* sedum album *'Coral Carpet'*.

(Below) Big blue American agaves.

(Above) Santolina laid out in a spiral design.

(Above) View of living room screen porch from
lower garden.

(Above) View of pool towards house with plantings of Yucca gloriosa, *aeonium, and* Crassula argenta.

(Right) View of the bedroom wing with plantings of American agave, Artemesia 'Powis Castle' and Agave huachachensis.

Richard Strauss House (1940)
Raphael Soriano, architect

On a gradually sloping wedge-shaped lot in Cheviot Hills, a suburb of West Los Angeles, the Richard Strauss House was elevated slightly on its lot to take advantage of the view toward a neighboring golf course. The single-story house is planned around a garden off the living room, studio, and bedroom to make the most of outdoor living in southern California. One of the original features included a patio, which is screened by frosted glass set in a steel frame to create a shadowy effect reminiscent of a Japanese shoji screen.

The owner, a well-known food critic, planted a culinary herb and vegetable garden next to the kitchen with the assistance of Los Angeles designer Michael Berman. The surrounding landscape became a sub-tropical garden with a mixed palette of grasses, bamboo, cacti and sculptural succulents that complement the clean horizontal lines of the modern house. The original lath house joining the house to the garage was removed and in its place an exotic fruit and flower garden of green papaya, apricot, and plumeria trees was planted. In the central courtyard, Berman designed a five-foot bronze dish—planted with lotus water lilies, papyrus, and water cabbage—which acts as a reflecting pool. Geometric planting beds filled with natives and drought-tolerant plants enhance the thin horizontal pattern of the redwood siding. In the interior courtyard, a fuschia-colored hibiscus provides a focal point next to a large pineapple guava tree (*Feijoa sellowiana*).

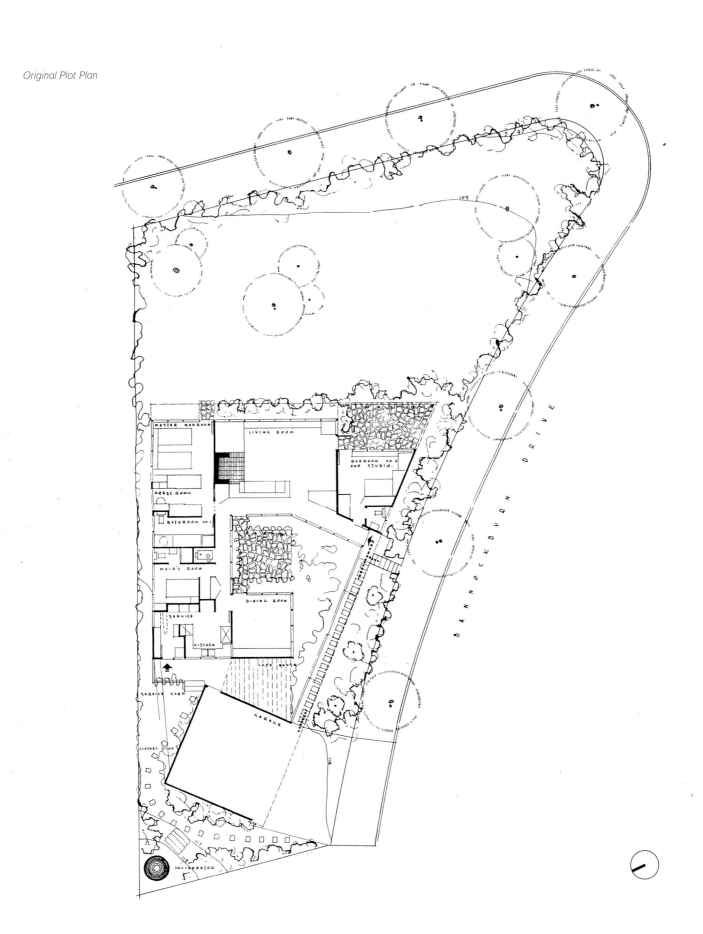

(Above, left) Early photo, night view of backlit glass screen.

(Above, right) Contemporary photo, day view of plantings with Yucca gloriosa, plumeria, *and* agave.

(Overleaf) Dining room courtyard with raised wood deck surrounded by lawn and planted with flax, papyrus, and roses.

Jack Shapiro House (1943/1948–49)
J.R. Davidson, architect

This one-story pavilion sits on a generous double lot in Los Angeles. The L-shape created by the two rectangular volumes of the house define a terrace that opens out on a diagonal to the swimming pool, surrounding hardscape, and the planting beds beyond. Every room has a relationship to the out-of-doors, especially the living room and master bedroom, which both open directly toward the pool. Entrance is gained by a curving path that leads to a gate opening onto an enclosed garden, the first room of the house. J.R. Davidson sited the house giving the entry court a west-facing exposure that allows the morning sun to spill into the living room.

The present owner, Kathy Guild, worked with landscape designer, Sarah Munster, to clarify the garden and create biomorphic shapes of concentrated areas of planting. For the entry court, Munster created a Japanese-inspired grass garden using stipa grass, juncus, variegated bamboo, and michelia tree. Around the pool the original shape of the hardscape was followed, though reduced in size. The enlarged crescent-shaped berm is planted with stipa grass. The swimming pool terrace is colorfully accented by restored pieces of mid-century garden furniture and pots from Architectural Pottery, a Los Angeles artisan cooperative that was active in the 1950s.

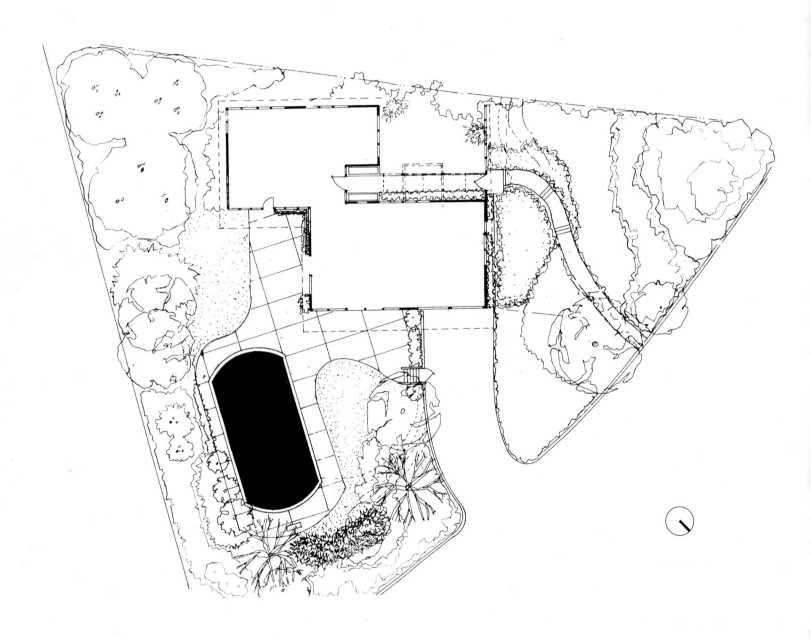

(Opposite top, left) Bamboo *and* Houtiuynia cordata *'Chameleon'.*

(Opposite top, right) Abutilon megapotanmicum savitzii.

(Opposite bottom, left) Ligularia *'Tussie Mussie' and in the rear,* Pittosporum tobira *'Variegata'.*

(Opposite bottom, right) Stipa gigantea.

(Above) House with variegated Boston ivy on the wall with Cyperus papyrus *and* Cyperus alternifolius.

(Left) View of garden from living room.

(Bottom) Seating area with potted succulents.

(Left) View of pool with tropical border.

(Below) Stipa grass with bench.

(Bottom) View of tropical border including three types of canna lilies, pelargonium, Loropetalum *'Razzle Dazzle'*, Asclepias tuberosa, *and* Salvia chiapensis.

Mar Vista Housing (1946–48)
Gregory Ain, architect

Mar Vista Housing was a very fruitful collaboration of an architect, landscape architect, and a developer in an effort to fill the need for post-war housing in southern California. One hundred homes were planned for a 60-acre site in Culver City and fifty-two were built. The original landscape architect, Garrett Eckbo, was responsible for addressing the public areas of the development—the sidewalks, parkways, street trees, and curbs. In an innovative manner, he pushed the sidewalks closer to the houses thereby creating a parkway that served as a place to plant street trees. To both unify the community and give each block a unique identity, Eckbo used a different species of tree for each street—magnolia on Meier, maleleuca on Moore, and ficus on Beethoven Street. The trees have matured and now provide a lush shaded canopy over the streets.

Half a century later, before retirement, Eckbo had the opportunity to design a landscape plan for a house renovated by Kevin Daly and Chris Genik of Daly-Genik, Architects. The design problem was to make an inviting garden out of a very small space that had shrunk after the house was expanded. The architects continued the modernist tradition of opening the house to the outdoors through slide-away glass corners. Eckbo added a poured concrete patio in a biomorphic shape to extend the living and dining areas into the garden. Foliage that is dark in color and dense in form was used to create depth perception, whereas the foliage of plants used in the foreground are shiny, variegated and lighter, tending to project forward. Eckbo also used an existing bamboo screen, which blocks out neighboring houses but still connects to the neighboring tree canopies, thereby creating the illusion of "borrowed landscape." He brought a pond up close to the house for reflected light to make the space seem even larger.

*(Right) Original Eckbo planting of dracenas,
c. 1950s.*

*(Bottom) Triangular steel posts become trellises
for vines at entrance, c. 1950s.*

(Left) View through breezeway entrance to streetscape, c. 1950s.

(Below, left) Garrett Eckbo, Mar Vista site plan. Rendered plan shows first phase of development; remainder was not developed.

(Below, right) Gregory Ain, Typical original plot plan.

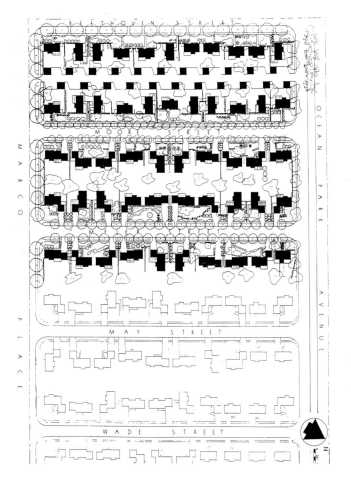

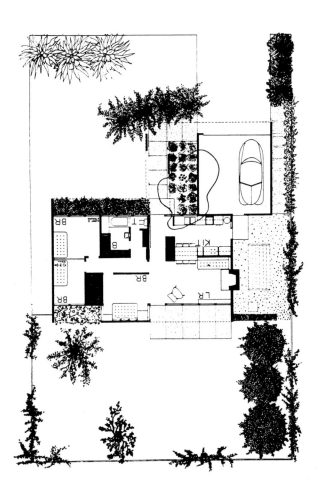

(Right, top and bottom) Garrett Eckbo's alternative designs for garden renovation.

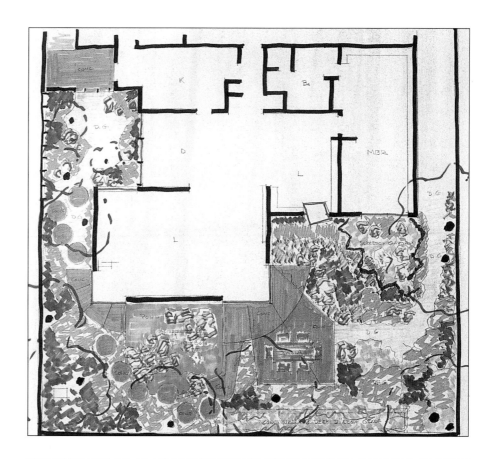

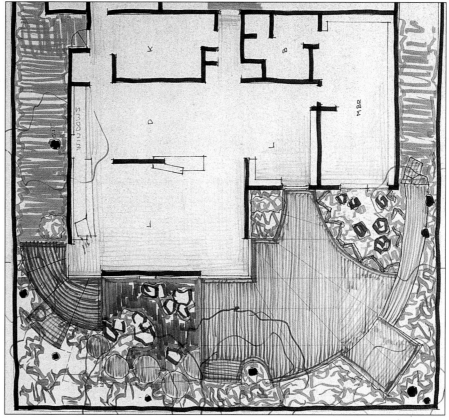

(Opposite) Patio off living room; reflecting pond planted with lilies and papyrus under the canopy of a corkscrew willow.

(Right) Front entry lawn with ferns, papyrus, flax.

(Bottom) Garden planted with gardenias and Abutilon megapotamicum with original Arbutus tree.

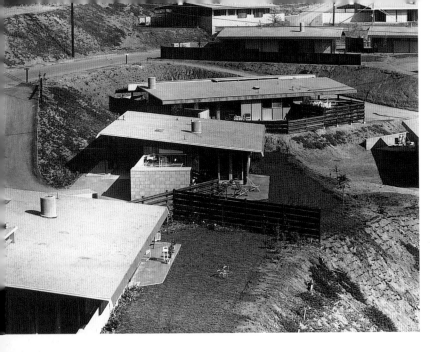

Robert Haas House (1948)
Whitney Smith and A. Quincy Jones, architects

Between 1946 and 1950, the Mutual Housing Association, a cooperative venture of 500 families (mainly made up of musicians, professionals in the film industry, and college professors) developed the hillside homes known as Crestwood Hills, sited on 800 acres in Brentwood. Robert Haas, a UCLA professor, chose one of the thirty-five plans designed by Whitney Smith and A. Quincy Jones. The nature of building on hillside terrain necessitated tremendous grading and reforming of all of the slopes into a series of stepped terraces or building pads. Garrett Eckbo collaborated with the architects to produce a site plan, which included a basic concept of using taller trees in the lower elevations of the canyons and broader, shorter trees for the ridges. Because Eckbo's plan, using regular spacing of street trees, was not implemented, the identity that landscape could provide is now lacking.

Cory Buckner, architect and recent owner of the Haas House, redesigned the garden with the addition of a small geometric swimming pool that aligns itself with the angles of the house. Surrounding the pool, Buckner introduced a semi-arid theme with echium and agave to help screen the pool from the carport. At the front entrance, horsetail (*Equisitum hyemale*) was planted to delineate the carport.

(Above, left) Patio seating area with butterfly chairs, flax and aloe in the background.

(Above, right) Pool.

(Bottom, left) Entry planted Festuca glauca and Equisetum hyemale.

(Bottom, right) Night view.

(Left) View from studio to patio with pond and succulent planting, c. 1950s.

(Opposite) Curtained courtyard with Shulman family and plantings of ficus tree and pansies, c. 1950s.

Julius Shulman House (1950)

Raphael Soriano, architect

Architect Raphael Soriano and landscape architect Garrett Eckbo joined with their client, architectural photographer Julius Shulman, to successfully collaborate on this hillside home. "Our site, extending in an east to westerly direction," Shulman explained, "offered an extensive view of ranges of hills to the south. This outlook, most desirable and satisfying to us, was the basis of Soriano's orientation and plan development." Because the house was sited parallel to the slope, it was possible to open it on the south and north sides to a series of patios, screened porches, and garden courts. By using sliding glass doors and screening material, Soriano created several transitional areas—recessed patios and projecting screened porches connected by a covered walkway on the south—to connect the indoors and outdoors. All of the major rooms—the living room, dining room, master bedroom, child's room and studio—extend out and partake of the landscape. The plant materials include bougainvillea, succulents, agapanthus, fortnight lily, and hanging geranium baskets. In addition, there are a series of outdoor rooms shaped by low retaining walls, plants and concrete paver walks that are carpeted with lawn and flowering ground covers.

(Top) Original site plan

(Bottom) Original Plot Plan

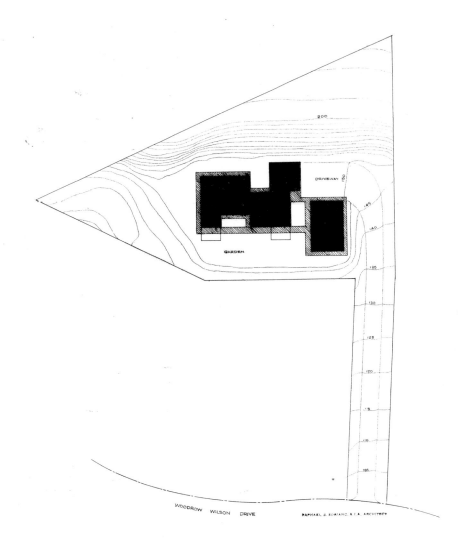

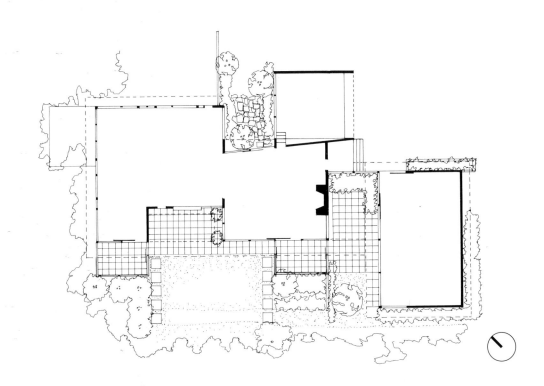

(Top) Screen porch with wisteria and irises.

(Middle) House wrapped with concrete paver pathway.

(Bottom) Agave attenuata *planted on hillside*

(Opposite) Brick path with camphor tree, wisteria, and ficus tree.

(Top) Screened dining porch with bougainvillea and hanging geraniums.

(Above) Potted succulents at garage entrance.

Albert Wohlstetter House (1953)

Joseph Van der Kar, architect

The architect sited this two-story house on a hillside in Laurel Canyon with an expansive view over a wooded valley of eucalyptus. The property is long, irregular, and steeply sloping, with the house sited between two ravines. The entrance is located on the uphill side, opening into the main living area. On the view side, a balcony cantilevers over the main garden terrace. This sometimes intimate, sometimes abstract landscape represents Garrett Eckbo's mature style at its finest. Its elements include geometric patterns of lawn and concrete paving, circular seating areas wrapped with wood benches, circular stepping stones, and constructed screens of fiberglass and other industrial materials. The garden includes three water features: a swimming pool, a small geometric fishpond, and a large metal disk which serves as a birdbath. Above the swimming pool on the east, a Reglex glass fence provides privacy from the street. A screen designed in the style of Piet Mondrian was used to camouflage the pool equipment.

(Above) Angular concrete patio looking west toward mountains, c. 1950s.

(Left) Plot Plan, c. 1955.

(Below) Later photo shows mature landscape and additional mosaic on amoeba-shaped concrete bench, 1966.

(Opposite) Earlier view of pool with dracenas and flax, c. 1950s. Fiberglas Mondrian-like paneled fence screens pool equipment.

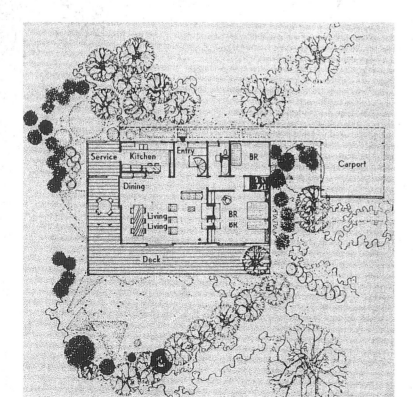

160

(Opposite, top) Garden with Fatsia japonica and bamboo.

(Opposite, bottom) Balcony above provides filtered light to garden below.

(Above) Golden bamboo screen provides backdrop for pool.

(Above) Water disk among bamboo with azaleas, liriope, and Fatsia japonica.

(Opposite) Lower concrete patio, round patio and circular wood bench enclosed by grove of timber bamboo.

165

A. Quincy Jones-
Frederick E. Emmons Office (1955)

A. Quincy Jones and Frederick E. Emmons, architects

Originally built as a one-story building and expanded in 1958 to two stories, the Jones-Emmons Office is one of the most refined small commercial buildings in West Los Angeles. One of the building's main elements is steel frame construction with floor-to-ceiling glass surrounding the interior courtyards. Jones and Emmons designed their office with special sensitivity so that all the work spaces relate to gardens. They gave as much attention to the proportion of the courtyards as to the offices.

Today the structure is owned by Frederick Fisher & Partners, who have preserved the building and continue it as an architect's office. Shortly after acquiring the building, landscape designer Jay Griffith refurbished several atrium gardens and recently Pamela Burton & Company redesigned the central courtyard around which the main circulation spaces and conference room are organized. An enormous existing eucalyptus tree and newly planted Japanese maple provide partial screening from the entry through the courtyard to the conference room. The square courtyard is composed of interlocking rectangles of river-washed pebbles and decomposed granite, framed by planted brackets of contrasting foliage of low growing shrubs. The color palette consists of burgundy (Chinese razzle-berry, red Japanese maple, and flax) contrasted with chartreuse foliage (asparagus and beaumontia vine). A bench inviting meditation completes the composition.

(Below) Streetscape showing mature plantings.

(Right) Original Plot Plan.

(Bottom) Pamela Burton, courtyard plan.

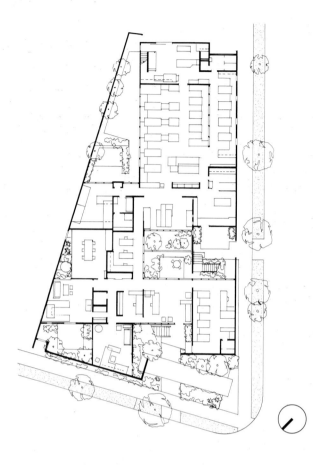

(Opposite, top left) Composition of textures: gravel, decomposed granite, and aggregate pavers.

(Opposite, top right) Flax 'Jack Sprat' frames view of walled garden.

(Opposite, bottom left) Burgundy cutleaf Japanese maple backed by Asparagas meyerii.

(Opposite, bottom right) View from conference room with Beaumontia vine on wall.

(Above) Private offices look out onto court planted with fiddleleaf fig and bamboo.

(Opposite) Weeping bamboo grows under skylight in conference room.

171

Gary Cooper House (1961)

A. Quincy Jones and Frederick E. Emmons, architects

With the recent renovation of the Gary Cooper House, the original landscaping by Eckbo, Royston, and Williams was addressed by Mark Rios and Associate, working along with the owners, David Bohnett and Tom Gregory. In order to maximize the garden spaces and to open the house to views of an adjacent wooded ravine, A. Quincy Jones and Frederick E. Emmons sited the Gary Cooper House as close to the street as possible. Spaces along the public face of the house are integrated with gardens. For instance, the main entry is set back under a canopy, with views of a garden composition which orchestrates a linear pond, a large Eckbo-designed planter dish overflowing with orchids, (*Epidendrum ibaguense*) and four existing lemon-scented gums (*Eucalyptus citriodora*).

Rios knitted the full length of the garden facing the ravine, in a linear composition with each of the main rooms opening onto it, while retaining the position of the swimming pool, the teahouse and the open lawn off the main bedroom. Rios sought to simplify and clarify in the spirit of the Eckbo garden. Drawing the visitor out into the garden spaces is a partially concealed wooden deck with a wisteria-covered trellis that juts out over the ravine.

Original Plot Plan

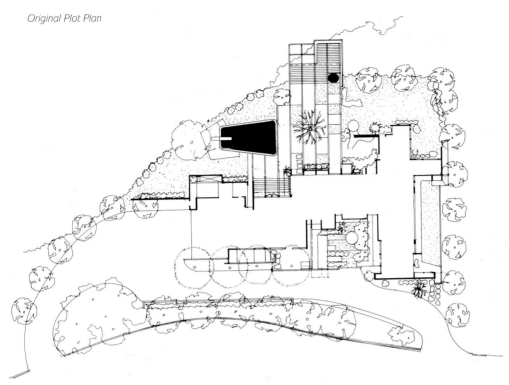

(Opposite, left) Mature ginkgo grove outside of living room.

(Opposite, right) At front entry, original metal dish replanted with epiphyllum.

(Opposite, bottom left) Jacaranda frames view of wood deck and trellis which the Cooper family called "the teahouse."

(Opposite, bottom right) Four remaining mature lemon gums are accompanied by spouts of chondropetalum and liriope.

Contemporary Plot Plan

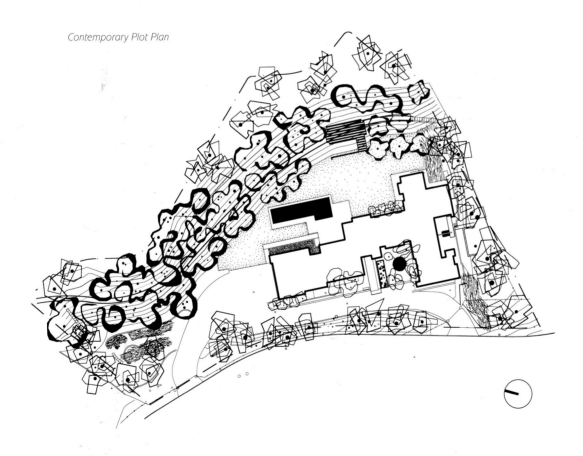

(Above) Comfortable chairs on the private wood deck with wisteria-covered trellis.

(Opposite, top) Rebuilt deck and trellis in the original design of Eckbo makes for a private retreat in the garden.

(Opposite, bottom left) Angular gravel walk planted with bamboo and liriope.

(Opposite, bottom right) Neatly-trimmed ficus against house surrounded by black/white pebbles.

(Above) View of pool. A former owner's rectangular shaped pool replaced Eckbo's original idea of a trapezoidal pool that forced the perspective.

(Opposite) View of pool and house.

Sheats-Goldstein House (1963)

John Lautner, architect

The Sheats-Goldstein House is located on a south-facing slope overlooking a canyon with sweeping views of the city and the ocean beyond. The second owner, James Goldstein, collaborated with the original architect, John Lautner, and landscape designer Eric Nagelman to expand the house and develop the garden into a spectacular tropical paradise.

The entry to the house is striking with a path leading to the front door through a garden where concrete, water, and glass are blended together in an unexpected way. Alocacia, fig, and Chinese elm inhabit the entry court. Plants grow out of the water and over the wall, with canopies cascading out of the sky. The view through walls of glass draws the visitor out to the pool terrace, a prow perched precipitously over the garden. The cantilever appears to continue to the horizon creating a feeling of danger as the visitor nears the edge unprotected by a handrail. From here, one returns to the house to descend into the garden. Beneath the precipice is a steeply sloping site where the only option for a garden was a series of pathways, twisting and turning with the terrain. There are periodic trapezoidal shelves used as miniature garden landings for viewing or resting, also serving as landmarks through the garden. Exotic, rare and unusual palms, giant bird of paradise and bananas, provide a sheltering microclimate for smaller plants and flowering ground cover such as tradescanthia, helconias, thunbergia vines, and bromeliads.

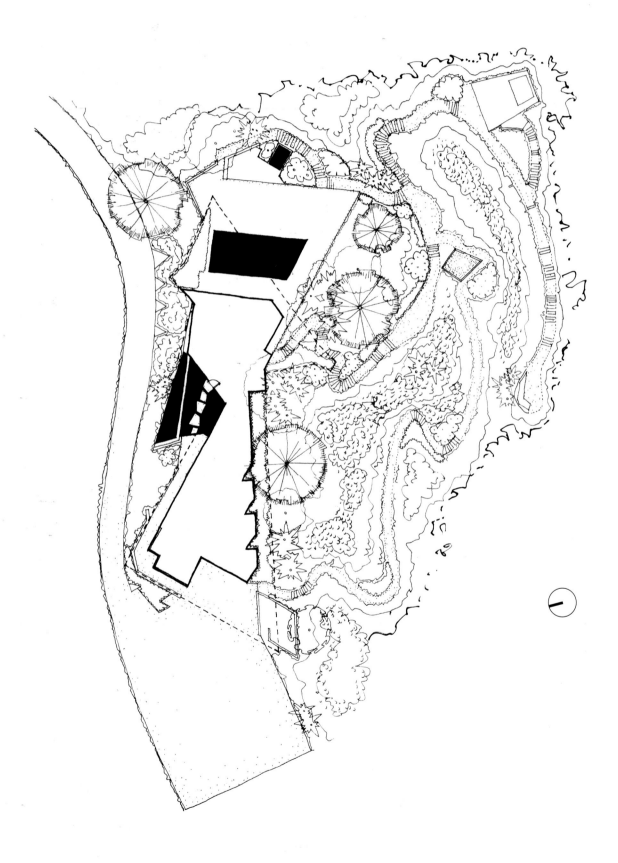

(Right) View from landing across banana and palm planting.

(Bottom) Cantilevered concrete steps lead to garden below.

(Above) Entry with view to pond through glass walls.

(Above) Trapezoidal stepping stones lead across entry pond.

(Opposite, top left) Giant bird of paradise.

(Opposite, top right) Kentia palm seeds.

(Opposite, bottom left) Fig fruits (Roxburghii) over entry pond.

(Opposite, bottom right) Inflorescence of bromeliad.

(Right) Dasylirion, tree fern and albino grass.

(Middle) Grouping of cycads with Tradescantia pallida 'Purpurea'.

(Bottom) Glass garden shelf cantilevers over ravine planted with palms.

(Overleaf) Tilted aggregate pool deck cantilevers out toward city. Underwater windows look into master bedroom.

Selected Bibliography

Dobyns, Winifred Starr. *California Gardens.* Foreword by Myron Hunt. New York: The MacMillan Company, 1931.

Drexler, Arthur and Thomas S. Hines. *The Architecture of Richard Neutra: From International Style to California Modern.* New York: The Museum of Modern Art, 1982.

Eckbo, Garrett. *Landscape for Living.* New York: An Architectural Record Book for Duell, Sloan, & Pearce, 1950.

_____. *The Art of Home Landscaping.* New York: McGraw-Hill, 1956.

Gebhard, David. *Schindler.* New York: Viking Press, 1971.

_____, with Harriette Von Breton and Lauren Weiss. *The Architecture of Gregory Ain: The Play Between the Rational and High Art.* Santa Barbara: UCSB Art Museum, 1980.

Germany, Lisa. *Harwell Hamilton Harris.* Austin: Center for the Study of American Architecture, 1985.

_____. *Harwell Hamilton Harris.* Foreword by Kenneth Frampton. Introduction by Bruno Zevi. Austin: University of Texas Press, 1991.

Hines, Thomas S. *Richard Neutra and the Search for Modern Architecture: A Biography and History.* New York and Oxford: Oxford University Press, 1982.

_____. *Irving Gill and the Architecture of Reform: A Study in Modernist Architectural Genius.* New York: Monacelli Press, 2000.

Kamerling, Bruce. *Irving Gill, Architect.* San Diego: San Diego Historical Society, 1993.

March, Lionel and Judith Sheine, editors. *R.M. Schindler: Composition and Construction.* London: Academy Editions, 1993.

McCoy, Esther. *Irving Gill, 1870-1936.* Los Angeles: Los Angeles County Museum in collaboration with The Art Center in La Jolla, 1958.

_____. *Five California Architects.* New York: Reinhold, 1960.

_____. *Case Study Houses, 1945-1962.* Second Edition. Los Angeles: Hennessey & Ingalls, Inc., 1977.

_____. *Vienna to Los Angeles: Two Journeys.* Foreword by Harwell Hamilton Harris. Santa Monica, California: Arts + Architecture Press, 1979.

_____. *The Second Generation.* Salt Lake City, Utah: Gibbs M. Smith, Inc., 1984.

Neutra, Richard. "Landscaping—A New Issue," in *Contemporary Landscape Architecture and Its Sources*, San Francisco, San Francisco Museum of Art, 1937.

_____. *Mystery and Realities of the Site.* Scarsdale, New York: Morgan & Morgan, 1951.

_____. *Life and Human Habitat.* Stuttgart: Verlagsanstalt Alexander Koch GMBH, 1956.

Padilla, Victoria. *Southern California Gardens: An Illustrated History.* Berkeley and Los Angeles: University of California Press, 1961.

Rosa, Joseph. *A Constructed View: The Architectural Photography of Julius Shulman.* New York: Rizzoli International, 1994.

Sarnitz, August. *R.M. Schindler, Architect: 1887-1953.* New York: Rizzoli International, 1988.

Serraino, Pierluigi and Julius Shulman. *Modernism Revisited.* Taschen, 2000.

Sheine, Judith. "R.M. Schindler, 10 Houses," in *2G*, III, 7, 4-127.

Smith, Kathryn. *Frank Lloyd Wright, Hollyhock House, and Olive Hill: Buildings and Projects for Aline Barnsdall.* New York: Rizzoli International, 1992.

_____. *Schindler House.* New York: Harry N. Abrams, 2001.

Treib, Marc and Dorothée Imbert. *Garrett Eckbo: Modern Landscapes for Living.* Berkeley and Los Angeles: University of California Press, 1997.

Acknowledgments

The research and documentation for this book owe much to the knowledge and generosity of a number of people and institutions.

First and foremost to the owners—some of whom wish to remain anonymous—who so graciously invited us into their gardens: Susan and Sidney Baldwin, Fred Fisher, Bella Francis, Benedict and Nancy Freedman, James Goldstein, Kathy Guild, Russ Leland, William Murphy and Mary Liebman, Rick and Eva Rossovich, Pippa Scott, Brian Tichenor and Raun Thorp, and Cliff Watts.

To the landscape architects, architects, and designers who shared their philosophy of design for mid-century gardens: Kevin Daly and Chris Genik, Steven Ehrlich, Frank Escher, Jay Griffith, Peter Gruenheisen, Leo Marmol and Ron Radziner, Sarah Munster, Eric Nagelman, Duncan Nicholson, Marc Rios, Brian Tichenor and Raun Thorp, and Joseph van de Kar. Further thanks to Liz Benbrooks, Samantha Harris, and Mark Tessier from the office of Mark Rios, and especially to Cory Buckner, whose help early on was invaluable.

A number of people at research facilities were exceedingly helpful. We wish to thank: Kurt G.F. Helfrich, curator, Architectural, Design, and Drawing Collection, University of California, Santa Barbara; Octavio Olvera and Jeff Rankin, Department of Special Collections, University of California, Los Angeles; Waverly Lowell, Environmental Design Archives, University of California, Berkeley; Douglas Silverstone and Lauren Bricker, Archives—Special Collections, College of Environmental Design, California State Polytechnic University, Pomona; Carol Bornstein, Santa Barbara Botanic Garden; and Mark Henderson, Getty Research Institute.

Special gratitude is extended to Julius Shulman, without whose extraordinary archives of photographs this book would not have been possible and whose knowledge and stories enriched our experience. Julius generously provided us with his personal understanding of the period. Special thanks to Judy McKee who, with such good humor, expedited and helped with her father's collections.

We extend our gratitude to the following who provided photographs or helped in the search: Russell A. Beatty, Benny Chan, Jack Coyier, John Ellis, Timothy Hursley, Elaine Jones, David Mason, Dion Neutra, Victoria Pearson, Jeremy Samuelson, Charles Sanchez, Tim Street-Porter, Marc Treib, Tom Vinetz, and Dominique Vorrillon.

We are grateful to special people who provided information or guidance: Mike Deasy, Susan Heeger, Thomas S. Hines, Barbara Lamprecht, Joe Molloy, Louise Sandhaus, Robert Sweeney, Sian Winship, and Aino Paasonen.

The support of the staff, and especially several individuals, at Pamela Burton & Company is greatly appreciated: Gabrielle Jennings, Marti Kyrk, Lisa Swanson, Patricia Moisan and Stephanie Psomas. To Chanon Billington we owe special thanks. Warm thanks for their past efforts to Robin Benezera, Katherine Spitz, Mary Sager McFadden, Steve Flood, Steve Billings, David Fletcher, and Tom Gibson.

James Trulove has been extraordinary to work with—always enthusiastic and understanding. It was his suggestion to put us in touch with James Pittman, whose design provides just the right note for mid-century modernism. We also wish to acknowledge the generous and insightful assistance of Kathryn Smith, without whom this book would never have been written, and who read the manuscript and made useful suggestions. Special thanks to Randall Kennon and Rusty for their patience, understanding, and entertainment.

Finally, we would like to thank both Richard Hertz and Bruce Botnick, who have remained our constant sounding boards on the subject of mid-century gardens. They have both been powerful supporters and patient sages throughout the gestation of this book.

Pamela Burton
Marie Botnick

Credits

Photography

RUSSELL BEATTY
74, 75, 76, 77

TOM BONNER
34T

MARIE BOTNICK
42T, 42B, 43T, 43B, 96MR, 96 BR, 141TR, 187T

CORY BUCKNER
151TL, 151TR

BENNY CHAN
27, 29

JACK COYIER
169TL, 169TR, 169BL, 169BR

GARRETT ECKBO
172, 143T (U.C. BERKELEY Environmental Design Archives)

JOHN ELLIS
58, 59, 60, 61, 62, 63, 64, 65

GRIFFITH GARDNER
151BL, 151BR

ELEANOR HAAS
90, 91T, 93T

LUCKHAUS STUDIOS
14, 32, 33, 35 (UCLA Special Collections)

DAVID MASON
91B, 93B

VICTORIA PEARSON
94, 95, 96TL, 96TR, 96BL, 97, 98, 99, 118, 119, 120T, 120B, 121, 122, 123, 124, 125

LISA ROMEREIN
147T

JEREMY SAMUELSON
50, 51L, 51R, 52, 53, 103T, 103BL, 103BR, 104, 105BR

JULIUS SHULMAN
BACK COVER, 15, 25R, 38, 39, 41, 44, 45, 47T, 47B, 48, 49, 54, 55, 57T, 57B, 66, 67, 69, 70, 71, 72, 73, 78, 79, 81T, 81B, 100, 101, 114, 116T, 116B, 117T, 117B, 126, 127, 129L, 132, 133, 142, 143, 144T, 148, 149, 152, 153, 155T, 155M, 155B, 156, 157T, 157B, 158, 159, 160T, 161, 180, 181

TIM STREET-PORTER
COVER, 1, 2, 3, 9, 13, 18, 19, 20, 21, 36T, 36BL, 36BR, 37T, 37B, 82, 83, 84, 85, 86, 87, 106, 107, 109 110L, 110R, 111L, 111R, 112, 113R, 135, 136TL, 136TR, 136BL, 136BR, 137, 138T, 138B 139, 140, 141BR, 167, 168TL, 170, 171, 173, 175TL, 175TR, 175BR, 175BL, 176T, 176BL, 176BR, 177, 178, 179, 183T, 183B, 184, 185, 186TL, 186TR, 186BL, 186BR, 187M, 187B, 188, 189

KATHRYN SMITH
10

MARC TREIB
160R

DOMINIQUE VORILLON
129R, 130, 131, 146, 147B, 162T, 162B, 163, 164, 165

Drawing/Illustration & Model Credits

PAMELA BURTON & CO.
27, 28T, 28M, 28B, 29, 34B, 40B, 46B, 56B, 80, 92, 108, 134, 150, 154B, 168BL

STEVEN ERLICH
34T-Model

ELAINE JONES
166, 168TR, 174T

DUNCAN NICHOLSON
182

MARC RIOS
88, 174B

JOSEF VAN DER KAR
160BL

UC Berkeley—Garrett Eckbo Collection, Environmental Design Archives
145T, 145B

UCLA—Department of Special Collections— Charles E. Young Research Library
24B, 26T, 26B, 30, 34M, 40T, 46T, 56T

College of Environmental Design California State Polytechnic University, Pomona, California
128, 154T

UCSB—Architectural Drawing Collection, University Art Museum, Santa Barbara
12, 20B, 24T, 102, 115T, 115B, 144BL, 144BR